CW00357927

the
Yorkshire Dales

Compiled by
Dennis and Jan Kelsall

Acknowledgements

The authors thank the staff of the Yorkshire Dales National Park Authority for their valuable help.

Text: Dennis and Jan Kelsall
Photography: Dennis and Jan Kelsall
Editorial: Ark Creative (UK) Ltd
Design: Ark Creative (UK) Ltd

© Crimson Publishing Ltd

 This product includes mapping data licensed from Ordnance Survey® with the permission of the Controller of Her Majesty's Stationery Office. © Crown Copyright 2012. All rights reserved. Licence number 150002047. Ordnance Survey, the OS symbol and Pathfinder are registered trademarks and Explorer, Landranger and Outdoor Leisure are trademarks of the Ordnance Survey, the national mapping agency of Great Britain.

ISBN: 978-1-85458-518-9

While every care has been taken to ensure the accuracy of the route directions, the publishers cannot accept responsibility for errors or omissions, or for changes in details given. The countryside is not static: hedges and fences can be removed, stiles can become gates, field boundaries can alter, footpaths can be rerouted and changes in ownership can result in the closure or diversion of some concessionary paths. Also, paths that are easy and pleasant for walking in fine conditions may become slippery, muddy and difficult in wet weather, while stepping stones across rivers and streams may become impassable.

If you find an inaccuracy in either the text or maps, please write to Crimson Publishing at the address below.

First published 2001 by Jarrold Publishing
Revised and reprinted 2006 and 2008.

This edition first published in Great Britain 2012 by Crimson Publishing
Westminster House, Kew Road
Richmond, Surrey, TW9 2ND
www.totalwalking.co.uk

Printed in Singapore. 4/12

A catalogue record for this book is available from the British Library.

Front cover: Low Straights Lane
Previous page: Across the field towards Hollins House

Contents

Keymap

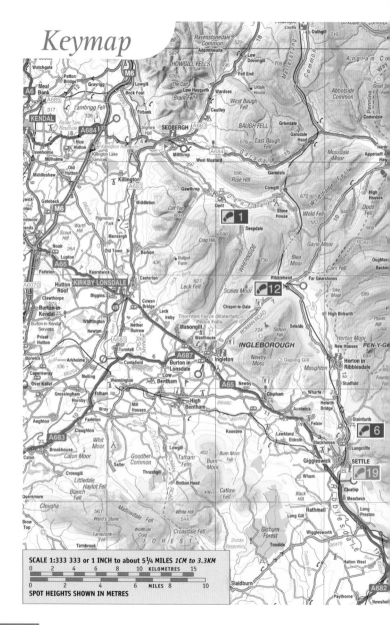

SCALE 1:333 333 or 1 INCH to about 5¼ MILES *1CM to 3.3KM*

0   2   4   6   8   10   KILOMETRES   15

0   2   4   6   MILES   8   10

SPOT HEIGHTS SHOWN IN METRES

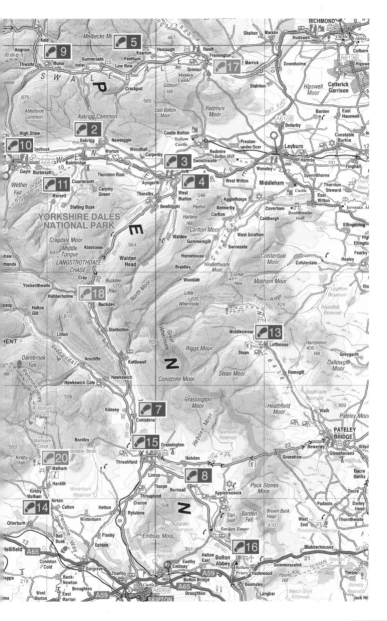

At-a-glance

1

Around Dent

2

Askrigg's Waterfalls

3

Aysgarth Falls

4

West Burton Falls and Morpeth Scar

• Wooded gorge • superb views • riverside walk • pretty village	• Interesting village • fine church • old limekiln • waterfalls	• Three waterfalls • scenic views • woodland • rural church	• Lovely village • waterfall • panoramic views • pretty woodland
Walk Distance 3 miles (4.8km) **Time** 1½ hours **Refreshments** Cafés and pubs in Dent, picnic area beside car park	**Walk Distance** 3¼ miles (5.2km) **Time** 1½ hours **Refreshments** Tearooms and pubs in Askrigg	**Walk Distance** 3 miles (4.8km) **Time** 1½ hours **Refreshments** Coppice Coffee Shop and Mill Race Tea Shop, picnic area by Upper Falls	**Walk Distance** 2¾ miles (4.4km) **Time** 1½ hours **Refreshments** Fox and Hounds at West Burton
Field paths and tracks; initial steep climb; stream crossing; narrow stiles	Field and woodland paths and tracks; narrow stiles; *steep drop beside path in gorge*	Woodland and field paths; *care needed beside waterfalls*	Field paths and tracks; sustained climb during early part of walk

Walk Completed ☑   Walk Completed ☐   Walk Completed ☐   Walk Completed ☐

5

Surrender Bridge and Old Gang Mill

6

Stainforth to Catrigg Force

7

Conistone Pie

8

Around Burnsall

• Heritage valley • ruined smelt mills • stone flues • old lead workings	• Wooded gorge • panoramic views • waterfall • stepping stones	• Dry gorge • clints • fine views • ancient church	• Splendid views • riverside walk • river cliffs • historic church

Walk Distance
3¼ miles (5.2km)

Time
1½ hours

Refreshments
Punch Bowl Inn at Feetham (1 mile)

Walk Distance
2½ miles (4km)

Time
1½ hours

Refreshments
Craven Heifer and picnic area in Stainforth

Walk Distance
3 miles (4.8km)

Time
1½ hours

Refreshments
Nearby, Kilnsey Park café and Tennant's Arms

Walk Distance
3 miles (4.8km)

Time
1½ hours

Refreshments
Wharfe View Tea Room and Red Lion in Burnsall

Broad tracks throughout

Field paths and tracks; sustained climb at start; *care needed beside waterfall*

Field paths and tracks; short and easy scrambles

Steep climb along field paths at beginning of walk; narrow suspension bridge

p.32

p. 36

p. 40

p. 44

Walk Completed ☐

Walk Completed ☐

Walk Completed ☐

Walk Completed ☐

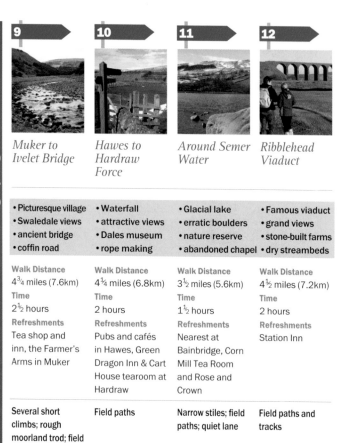

9	10	11	12
Muker to Ivelet Bridge	*Hawes to Hardraw Force*	*Around Semer Water*	*Ribblehead Viaduct*

• Picturesque village • Swaledale views • ancient bridge • coffin road	• Waterfall • attractive views • Dales museum • rope making	• Glacial lake • erratic boulders • nature reserve • abandoned chapel	• Famous viaduct • grand views • stone-built farms • dry streambeds
Walk Distance 4¾ miles (7.6km) **Time** 2½ hours **Refreshments** Tea shop and inn, the Farmer's Arms in Muker	**Walk Distance** 4¼ miles (6.8km) **Time** 2 hours **Refreshments** Pubs and cafés in Hawes, Green Dragon Inn & Cart House tearoom at Hardraw	**Walk Distance** 3½ miles (5.6km) **Time** 1½ hours **Refreshments** Nearest at Bainbridge, Corn Mill Tea Room and Rose and Crown	**Walk Distance** 4½ miles (7.2km) **Time** 2 hours **Refreshments** Station Inn
Several short climbs; rough moorland trod; field paths	Field paths	Narrow stiles; field paths; quiet lane	Field paths and tracks

p. 48	p. 53	p. 57	p. 61
Walk Completed ☑	Walk Completed ☐	Walk Completed ☐	Walk Completed ☐

13	14	15	16

Lofthouse to How Stean Gorge	*Kirkby Malham to Airton*	*Grassington to Grass Wood*	*Wharfedale, Barden Tower and The Strid*
• Pleasant riverside • Nidderdale views • hill-top church • mini canyon	• Attractive village • riverside path • Pennine Way • interesting church	• Lively village • folk museum • woodland reserve • riverside walk	• Woodland • lovely riverside • Barden Tower • The Strid
Walk Distance 3½ miles (5.6km)	**Walk Distance** 3¾ miles (6km)	**Walk Distance** 5 miles (8km)	**Walk Distance** 5 miles (8km)
Time 1½ hours	**Time** 2 hours	**Time** 2½ hours	**Time** 2½ hours
Refreshments Crown Hotels at both Lofthouse and Middlesmoor and café at How Stean Gorge	**Refreshments** Victoria pub at Kirkby Malham, Town End Farm tearoom at Airton	**Refreshments** Café at Information Centre, cafés and pubs in Grassington	**Refreshments** Cafés near car park and at Barden Tower, picnic tables
Field paths; climb to Middlesmoor	Field paths and trods	Generally clear paths and tracks	Riverside and undulating woodland paths

| p.65 | p. 69 | p. 73 | p. 78 |

| Walk Completed ☐ | Walk Completed ☐ | Walk Completed ☐ | Walk Completed ☐ |

17

18

19

20

Reeth to Marrick Abbey	*Buckden to Hubberholme*	*Settle to Victoria and Jubilee Caves*	*Malham Cove, Gordale Scar & Janet's Foss*
• Folk museum • valley views • site of abbey • earthworks	• Excellent views • Karst scenery • ancient church • stepping stones	• Wild moorland • caves • geological fault • interesting town	• Great scenery • resurgence • dry valley • waterfalls
Walk Distance 6 miles (9.7km)	**Walk Distance** 5 miles (8km)	**Walk Distance** 5¼ miles (8.4km)	**Walk Distance** 5 miles (8km)
Time 3 hours	**Time** 2½ hours	**Time** 3 hours	**Time** 2½ hours
Refreshments Choice of pubs and tearooms in Reeth, and the Bridge Inn at Grinton	**Refreshments** Café and Buck Inn in Buckden, White Lion Inn at Cray, George Inn at Hubberholme	**Refreshments** Choice of cafés and pubs in Settle, picnic area above Upper Settle	**Refreshments** Several cafés and two pubs, Listers Arms Hotel and Buck Inn in Malham
Sustained climb along quiet lane; field paths and tracks	Sustained climb; field paths; stepping stones	Sustained climb; tracks and field paths	Field paths; steep, stepped path; *unguarded cliffs and slippery rocks*

Walk
Completed ☑

Walk
Completed ☐

Walk
Completed ☐

Walk
Completed ☐

Introduction

The Yorkshire Dales

For the walker, coming to the Yorkshire Dales for the first time is like an initial chance meeting with a person who later becomes a lifelong friend: there is an immediate rapport, but also a sense of something much deeper that will take time to unearth. And like people, the Dales have many characteristics that alter day by day, changing with the seasons, the weather and the hour. As with a friend, a lifetime can never be enough to discover all.

High moors and gentle valleys

Set fairly in the middle of the great Pennine chain that sweeps through Northern England, the Yorkshire Dales has a quality not found elsewhere. It is a distinction reflected in its people, their traditions and the villages in which they live, and is a product, at least in part, of the unique landscape. Although the region encompasses vast expanses of high, lonely moor and has many respectable hills worthy of ascent, it is the intricate web of gentle valleys that gives the area its name, the Dales.

Uplift and erosion have created a highly varied landscape, full of interest and beauty, founded predominantly on limestone and grit. From wet upland bog to lush riverside meadows, green valleys to stark defiles, and grey cliffs to verdant woodland, every walk offered here unfolds as a changing vista.

The ice ages have been crucial in moulding the landscape, creating the extensive limestone pavements that appear in the south west. Even in retreat, the ice left its mark, in drumlins, moraines and strange erratic boulders, stranded as aliens in a foreign country. And the massive torrents of water, released by melting ice, cut rocky ravines on a scale irreconcilable with the becks now flowing at their base. The process continues, and the many spectacular waterfalls,

The Ribblehead Viaduct remains a tribute to its Victorian builders

so often the focus for a walk, remain a testament to the power of the water, slowly cutting back the lips over which they tumble. Rainfall has a more subtle action, imperceptibly dissolving the limestone along its cracks and fissures to create enigmatic features that characterise limestone country: grikes, gaping holes and disappearing rivers – the portals to a mysterious world below ground.

Changing ways of life

Farming has ever been the mainstay of economic activity in the Dales, and a major instrument of man's own contribution to the moulding of the landscape. Thousands of miles of drystone wall divide the wide valleys into a patchwork of neat fields, while the hillsides are scoured by an innumerable population of nibbling sheep. Mining for lead and zinc ore as well as coal and quarrying for stone have been important industries too. Quarrying still continues in places. But mining has ceased and after its heyday during the late 18th and 19th centuries, the output from these remote workings was unable to match imported metal prices. The gaunt remains of the pitheads and smelt mills now lie derelict upon the high moors, a place to pause, take out your flask and let your imagination run free.

Ever since the first Norse settlers introduced sheep to the area, textiles have played a significant role. In medieval times, huge tracts of open land were put to sheep runs by their monastic owners. The export of wool generated vast incomes for the abbeys and turned many of the villages into busy market centres. Spinning and weaving developed as cottage industries and, as the factory system emerged, the fast-flowing rivers were harnessed to power mills. More important in some areas was knitting, often undertaken by every member within a community. However, the advent of steam power and the machinery of the Industrial Age took the work away.

Yet, as one door closed another opened as the spreading tentacles of the railway heralded the dawn of a new industry, tourism. The beauties of the landscape had already been extolled by early Victorian artists and poets and now, for the first time, cheap, convenient transport brought them within reach of ordinary people. Workers and their families from the surrounding industrial towns flocked to the Dales as both day-trippers and holidaymakers. As today, many came simply as sightseers, but the more energetic and adventurous established a tradition of exploratory rambling for which the region is so popular today.

Network of paths and trackways
Although apparently remote, even before the coming of the turnpikes in the 18th century, the area was well served by a network of paths and trackways. From man's earliest incursions, tracks snaked into the hills and, as settlements spread into the valleys after the Roman period, so did the paths. The medieval period saw a proliferation of communication, with new routes springing up connecting the monastic houses with their extensive estates, remote granges and markets. Added to this were the tracks established by drovers, bringing Scottish cattle to English markets. Many traditional routes remain, the basis for the network of footpaths and

bridleways enjoyed by today's walkers and, with over 1,100 miles of them criss-crossing the hills and dales of the National Park, there is no lack of opportunity to explore in the finest way – on foot.

The walks in this book are suggested as an introduction to the many aspects of this wonderful area and help you explore some of the rich legacy that nature, history, occupation and industry have imparted. From the gentle landscape and wooded valleys of the lower dales to the splendid isolation and stark beauty of the encompassing hills, there is something new at every turn. In the villages too there is much to see, with the buildings often reflecting different periods of their prosperity. Many have small museums that interpret the area's natural and social histories, and do not forget to look around the churches, which in many ways have maintained the spirit of village life over the centuries.

Planning your walk
The walks are graded by length and difficulty and if you, or your children have not walked before, choose from the easier walks for your first outings. But note that the Dales landscape is far from flat and even the shorter routes usually involve brief climbs.

Many of the walks lend themselves to variation and consideration of the map will often suggest a shorter or longer ramble. Remember that the countryside is a living and working entity and is constantly changing. Landmarks can disappear, stiles may be replaced by gates and even rights of way are occasionally altered. However, attention to the route descriptions, reference to the maps and a little common sense will get you around without trouble.

An indication of what to expect along the way is given under the 'Route Features' for each walk, but the precise nature of the ground underfoot will depend upon the season and recent weather conditions; limestone can be very slippery when wet, paths can be muddy at any time of the year and luxuriant summer vegetation means that shorts are not always a good idea.

Neat walls and laithes

The times given suggest how long the 'average' person might take, but make no allowance for stops along the way. Individual performance will vary and be affected by many things. If you do set out on a walk and discover that the going is harder than expected, the weather has deteriorated or you are simply taking longer than you anticipated, do not be afraid to turn back. The route will always be there for another day, when you are fitter, the children are more experienced or the weather is kinder.

This book includes a list of waypoints alongside the description of the walk, so that you can enjoy the full benefits of gps should you wish to.

For more information on using your gps, read the *Pathfinder® Guide GPS for Walkers*, by gps teacher and navigation trainer, Clive Thomas (ISBN 978-0-7117-4445-5).

For essential information on map reading and basic navigation, read the *Pathfinder® Guide Map Reading Skills* by outdoor writer, Terry Marsh (ISBN 978-0-7117-4978-8). Both titles are available in bookshops or can be ordered online at www.totalwalking.co.uk

Around Dent

- Wooded gorge
- superb views
- riverside walk
- pretty village

walk 1

Although beginning steeply up Flinter Gill, the ascent is soon accomplished and the effort compensated with stunning views to the Howgills. After wandering between hillside farms, the route ambles along the banks of the Dee. Back in Dent, visit St Andrew's Church or look for the massive block of granite commemorating the Victorian geologist Adam Sedgwick.

The view to the head of Dentdale

walk 1

START Dent

DISTANCE 3 miles (4.8km)

TIME 1½ hours

PARKING Car park in village (Pay and Display)

ROUTE FEATURES Field paths and tracks; initial steep climb; stream crossing; narrow stiles

GPS WAYPOINTS
SD 704 870
Ⓐ SD 701 864
Ⓑ SD 709 863
Ⓒ SD 715 860
Ⓓ SD 715 865
Ⓔ SD 715 867

PUBLIC TRANSPORT None

REFRESHMENTS Cafés and pubs in Dent, picnic area beside car park

PUBLIC TOILETS Adjoining the car park

PLAY AREA By the village green, passed early in the walk

ORDNANCE SURVEY MAPS Explorer OL2 (Yorkshire Dales – Southern & Western areas), Landranger 98 (Wensleydale & Upper Wharfedale)

Take the lane opposite the car park entrance beside Dent Memorial Hall, later keeping ahead at a sign to Flinter Gill past the village green. Once part of a packhorse route to Lancaster, the way becomes a stone track as it leaves the village, steepening alongside the wooded gorge of the gill.

Partway up, just beyond a second gate and a restored limekiln Ⓐ, bear left off the track onto a less distinct path, which leads into the gully of Flinter Gill. Tumbling over wide, flat slabs, the stream can normally be crossed with ease, but *take care as the wet rocks may be slippery*. Climb to a stile above the opposite bank and head back downhill. In the second rough field, a track develops, which drops to leave beside a cottage at the bottom.

Immediately past the cottage, turn right at a sign pointing across the fields towards Coventree. Entering the third field, make for a gated stile in the top wall, just left of a barn. From there, a hedged path falls to a junction above a cottage, West Banks. Ignoring the

> In the 18th century, Dent prospered from both farming and quarrying, and just about everybody contributed to the other main industry, **knitting**. Not a moment was lost to the task, with social groups gathering every evening to gossip, read aloud and tell stories, all to the accompaniment of clicking needles.

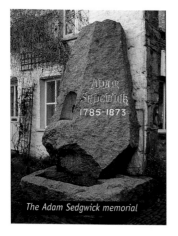

The Adam Sedgwick memorial

crossing track, pass through a pinch-stile in the opposite wall and stride on towards an abandoned cottage, visible through the trees ahead.

Walk in front of the old farmhouse to find a narrow stile, just right of a barn. Continue over the fields to intercept a track above East Banks Farm **B**. Cross and maintain your direction above the farm buildings towards yet another farm, Near Helks. Join a concrete track into the farmyard and walk past the farmhouse. As it then bends left, keep ahead towards the cottages at Far Helks. Pass behind them and bear left across the field beyond, dropping to a stile in the far corner. Carry on above a wooded gully to a gate, through which, go right to a footbridge. Follow the path away to come out onto a lane at Coventree **C**.

Walk left to a junction and cross to a track beside a cottage opposite, signed Double Croft Lane. Follow that down to Double Croft Cottage

Above Flinter Gill

D, but instead of turning in, go through a gate ahead along the continuation of the track to the River Dee **E**.

The lower track is subject to flooding and may occasionally be impassable. In which case, it will be necessary to return to

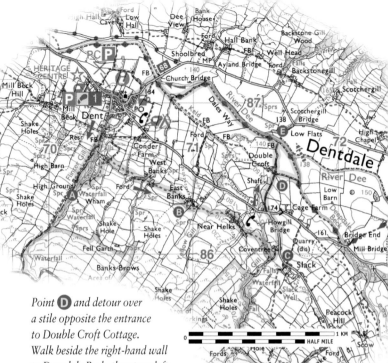

Point **D** and detour over a stile opposite the entrance to Double Croft Cottage. Walk beside the right-hand wall to Deepdale Beck, then turn left and follow it down to the Dee, continuing ahead to rejoin the main route at **E**.

Head downstream beside the Dee. Eventually, the way parts company with the river, following the field-edge to a slab bridge spanning Keld Beck. Once over, follow the stream right to its confluence with the Dee at Church Bridge. Climb out to a lane and go left back to Dent. In the village, swing right in front of the church to return to the car park.

■

? The floor of St Andrew's chancel is paved in Dent marble. What can you see embedded in the stone?

✱ One of the loveliest churches in the area, **St Andrew's** still retains box pews, identified with the names of the families who occupied them. The pulpit was once a fine Jacobean three-decker affair and the nearby master's desk came from the village school.

Askrigg's Waterfalls

- ■ Interesting village
- ■ fine church
- ■ old limekiln
- ■ gorge and waterfalls

walk 2

A short climb from Askrigg leads to an old moorland lane, giving magnificent views across Herriot's Wensleydale. The way back follows a woodland path past Whitfield Gill Force to Mill Gill Falls, where you can detour to the foot of the spectacular cascade before returning to the village.

Sykes's House in Askrigg

walk 2

🥾 Leave Market Place beside St Oswald's churchyard, walking along Main Street into Mill Lane. After 200 yds, just beyond a snaking bend, look on the right for a discretely marked footpath leaving beside house garages Ⓐ. Pass to the field behind and head to its far left corner. Continue by the wall towards a laithe, just before which, cross a stile. Cut left to a second stile and head to a gap-stile in the top wall.

> ✳ Served by the Richmond to Lancaster turnpike and, later, the railway, **Askrigg** was once an important town whose industries included dying, spinning, hand-knitting and clock-making. Askrigg's former prosperity is reflected in St Oswald's Church, the biggest in the dale. The magnificent beamed roof above its nave is considered to be one of the finest in the county.

Bear left to a gate in the corner above a barn and head out along an irregularly shaped field to find a stile 50 yds short of its far-left corner. Keep the same line to a wall gap and then climb a final field to emerge beside a gate onto a track, Low Straights Lane Ⓑ.

Follow it uphill to its end, where a sign marks a path to Mill Gill and Helm Ⓒ. Falling towards a wooded gorge above Whitfield Gill Force, the way remains at the rim before later winding down to a bridge spanning the stream. Climb left, soon reaching a junction where a path on the right leads back to end

Mill Gill Falls

above the waterfall. Unfortunately, although the sound of the cascade drifts from below, the view is largely obscured by trees.

Return to the junction and continue down the valley, later breaking into a meadow. At a four-way sign, keep ahead towards Mill Gill over a stile. The path rises beside a wall, but after 50 yds, crosses back into the trees. Lower down, ignore a path signed over a bridge and instead slip through a gap on the right to bypass a narrow ravine at the field-edge. In the second field, look for a squeeze-stile back into the wood. Descending within the trees, watch for a trod just before a junction that cuts back sharp left to a substantial limekiln. From the junction itself **D**, a path runs up the valley

> The 65-foot drop of **Mill Gill Falls** into a narrow, wooded gorge can be a stunning sight after prolonged rain. With the opening of the Wensleydale Railway, it became a popular Victorian beauty spot. The nearby **limekiln** is one of many scattered throughout the Dales. Generally dating from the 18th century, they were built to burn the stone to produce fertiliser.

below the kiln to the foot of the impressive Mill Gill Falls.

Continue with the main path down the valley, briefly returning to the adjacent meadow before swinging back to a bridge across the river. Follow the stream to an abandoned mill, there winding beneath an aqueduct that once supplied the wheel. Emerging into a field, take the flagged path out to Mill Lane and go left back to the village. ■

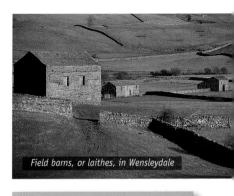

Field barns, or laithes, in Wensleydale

? Look for an iron ring embedded in the ground by the village cross. What was its purpose?

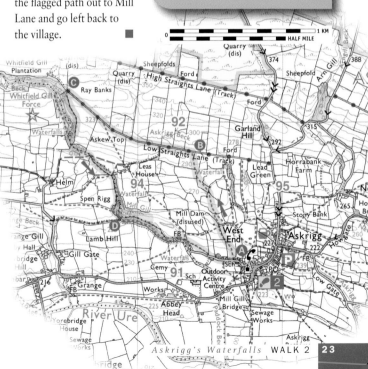

Aysgarth Falls

- Three waterfalls
- scenic views
- ancient woodland
- rural church

walk 3

After passing Aysgarth's Middle and Lower Falls, the walk rises across open farmland above the Ure. There are excellent views across Wensleydale before returning through the ancient woodland of Freeholders' Wood. A short walk in the other direction leads to the Upper Falls and nearby St Andrew's Church.

Across the fields towards Hollins House

walk **3**

START Aysgarth
Falls National Park
Information Centre

DISTANCE 3 miles (4.8km)

TIME 1½ hours

PARKING Car park
at National Park
Information Centre (Pay
and Display)

ROUTE FEATURES
Woodland and field
paths; *care needed
beside waterfalls*

GPS WAYPOINTS
SE 011 887
Ⓐ SE 016 888
Ⓑ SE 020 895
Ⓒ SE 016 891
Ⓓ SE 010 885

PUBLIC TRANSPORT
Bus service between
Northallerton and Hawes

REFRESHMENTS
Coppice Coffee Shop
in Information Centre
and Mill Race Tea Shop
overlooking Yore Bridge,
picnic area by Upper Falls

PUBLIC TOILETS Adjoining
Information Centre

PLAY AREA None

ORDNANCE SURVEY MAPS
Explorer OL30
(Yorkshire Dales –
Northern & Central
areas), Landranger 98
(Wensleydale & Upper
Wharfedale)

From the Information Centre, leave the car park along a footpath beside the entrance and follow the road right. At the end, cross to a gate into Freeholders' Wood. Bearing right, take a path signed to Middle and Lower Falls, shortly reaching steps on the right to a viewing platform above the Middle Falls.

Below Aysgarth village, the **River Ure** descends through a narrow, wooded gorge, dropping 200 feet in only ½ mile. After heavy rain, the river thunders in a boiling torrent over successive limestone steps, the famous Aysgarth Falls.

How and when were the rocks beneath your feet formed?

Return to the main path and continue through the wood. Passing through a gate, carry on past the return path rising from the Lower

Aysgarth's Upper Falls

Aysgarth Falls WALK 3   **25**

Falls. Later becoming stepped, the way falls to a junction. Turn sharp right to emerge on a rocky shelf above the Lower Falls.

Just upstream, a waymarker guides you through the trees back to the main path. Turn right as if to repeat the loop, but after 20 yds, bear left onto a grass path signed to Castle Bolton and Redmire **A**. At the end of a fence on the left, go through a hand-gate into an open field. Walk on towards Hollins House Farm, seen in the middle distance. A developing grass track leads through gates into the farm. Keep going past the barns and farmhouse, the way curving left into the fields beyond.

After a few yards, at a signpost, leave through the second of two adjacent gates on the right. Follow a trod at the field-edge to a gap-stile, but without crossing, swing left across the field to a gate near its western corner. Rejoining the track, go right. Just before a gate **B**, a path is signed off left along the bed of the former Wensleydale Railway to Aysgarth.

Emerging through a gated squeeze-stile, walk ahead across a large pasture. At the far side, turn left down a track dipping beneath the

Leaving established natural woodland on the route in late autumn

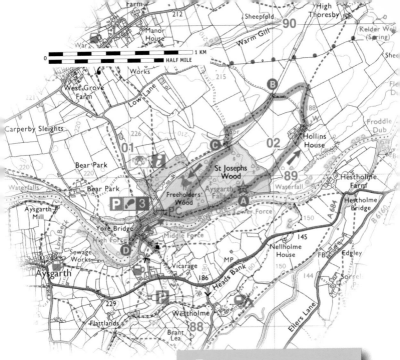

railway embankment into St Josephs Wood **C**. At a marker just ahead, bear right into the woodland, now becoming well established. Shortly, cross a stile into Freeholders' Wood and continue on an undulating path. At the

> ✴ So called because medieval freeholders enjoyed 'estover', the right to gather wood, **Freeholders' Wood** is a remnant of the broad-leaved forest that originally filled the valley. It is once again managed in the traditional method of coppicing, where the trees are periodically cut back to a stool, thus providing a regular supply of small timber.

end, leave through the gate by which you first entered the wood and turn right, back to the car park.

The Upper Falls **D** are easily reached along a short footpath from the far end of the car park. There is a small charge, but the meadow overlooking the falls is a fine spot for a picnic. St Andrew's Church lies across the bridge, and is reached by a stepped path beside Yore Mill. ∎

West Burton Falls and Morpeth Scar

- Charming village
- delightful waterfall
- panoramic views
- pretty woodland

walk 4

Although the first section of the walk involves a strenuous climb, it is not difficult and the height gained reveals magnificent views across Bishopdale and Wensleydale. The way back lies along an old track, Morpeth Gate, and then a woodland path, allowing a second view of the splendid waterfall before returning to the village.

Dropping to Morpeth Gate

walk 4

START West Burton

DISTANCE 2¾ miles
(4.4km)

TIME 1½ hours

PARKING Roadside
parking around village
green

ROUTE FEATURES Field
paths and tracks;
sustained climb during
early part of walk

GPS WAYPOINTS
🖉 SE 017 866
Ⓐ SE 021 867
Ⓑ SE 026 865
Ⓒ SE 029 879
Ⓓ SE 022 872

PUBLIC TRANSPORT
Bus service between
Northallerton and Hawes

REFRESHMENTS Fox and
Hounds at West Burton

PUBLIC TOILETS Nearest
public toilets at Aysgarth
Falls

PLAY AREA None

ORDNANCE SURVEY MAPS
Explorer OL30
(Yorkshire Dales –
Northern & Central
areas), Landranger 98
(Wensleydale & Upper
Wharfedale)

Like many Dales villages, the cottages of West Burton cluster around its **village green**, but this must be one of the largest in the whole country. The **village cross** is also unusual, an octagonal, stepped base topped by a pyramidal cap. It was only built in 1820 but probably replaced a much earlier market cross, since a large weekly market was once held on the site.

From the village cross, walk down beside the green. Where the lane bends in front of Mill House, swing right along a track towards the West Burton Falls. Over the packhorse bridge, just below the waterfall, climb steps out of the gorge. Turn right on a contained path and continue beyond its end to a stile at the corner of Barrack Wood Ⓐ.

? *What is the distinctive feature of a packhorse bridge?*

Climb within the perimeter fence to a squeeze-stile in the top wall and carry on up a scrubby bank. Over a fence-stile at the top, bear right to a break in the opposite boundary. Avoiding a direct assault of the steep slope, the path rises first left and then right to reach a stile in the top wall. With the worst of the ascent now behind you, keep going across open moorland, making for a large cairn that soon comes into view below a distant wall. Not far past the cairn is a stone track **B**, which to the left leads to Morpeth Scar.

Gently losing height, there is a magnificent panorama sweeping the foot of Bishopdale across Wensleydale to Bolton Castle. Beyond a ladder-stile, the descent gradually steepens, eventually dropping to a junction with another track, Morpeth Gate **C**. Turn left, walking for a good ½ mile and passing paths off on the right marked to Templars Chapel and

Swaledale sheep, bred for the hills

Temple Farm. About 200 yds beyond the second one, look for a path hidden in the trees on the left. It is signed to West Burton via Barrack Wood **D**.

Undulating under the trees, the way ultimately returns to the stile by which you originally entered the wood **A**. Retrace your outward steps across the fields and back down past the waterfall to the village. ∎

West Burton's village green is one of the largest in England

Surrender Bridge and Old Gang Mill

- ■ Heritage valley
- ■ ruined smelt mills
- ■ stone flues
- ■ old lead workings

During the 18th and 19th centuries, lead mining was a major industry in the Dales. Few sites are as impressive as the confined valley of Hard Level Gill, where countless mines and pits fed thundering processing mills. This walk explores the ruins of Surrender Bridge and Old Gang, evoking a vivid image of the massive scale on which the enterprise was undertaken.

walk 5

Surrender Bridge

START	Surrender Bridge
DISTANCE	3¼ miles (5.2km)
TIME	1½ hours
PARKING	Roadside parking area above Surrender Bridge
ROUTE FEATURES	Broad tracks throughout

GPS WAYPOINTS

SD 989 998
Ⓐ NY 990 000
Ⓑ SD 990 999
Ⓒ SD 989 999
Ⓓ NY 974 005

PUBLIC TRANSPORT None

REFRESHMENTS Punch Bowl Inn at Feetham (1 mile)

PUBLIC TOILETS None

PLAY AREA None

ORDNANCE SURVEY MAPS
Explorer OL30 (Yorkshire Dales – Northern & Central areas), Landrangers 92 (Barnard Castle) and 98 (Wensleydale & Upper Wharfedale)

One of the richest concentrations of the Dales' **lead deposits** lay beneath the hillsides enclosing Swaledale and was exploited in an almost unbroken string of mines that stretched eight miles between Swinner Gill and Hurst. Transporting ore was uneconomic and smelt mills were built in many of Swaledale's side valleys to turn it into metal.

From the parking area by the road junction, walk down to Surrender Bridge and continue up the lane for a further 200 yds towards a bridleway sign. Just beyond is a low tunnel burrowing beneath the road Ⓐ, part of a flue that took poisonous gases from the furnaces situated by the stream. Follow its line down the hillside to the smelt mill buildings Ⓑ.

To what temperature was the ore heated in the furnaces to produce lead?

Walk along the main track back to the lane at Surrender Bridge. Go right and almost immediately left onto a barriered track Ⓒ. Follow it into the narrowing valley for 1½ miles to the even more extensive remains of Old Gang Mill Ⓓ, which shortly come into view.

The track carries on up the valley for a further ½ mile to a junction at Level House Bridge, the narrower right fork continuing by the head stream to climb onto the hillside below Great Pinseat. The additional walk is not difficult and reveals the enormous extent of the mining activity in this area. The way back to Surrender Bridge simply retraces your outward track down the valley. ■

Old Gang Mill

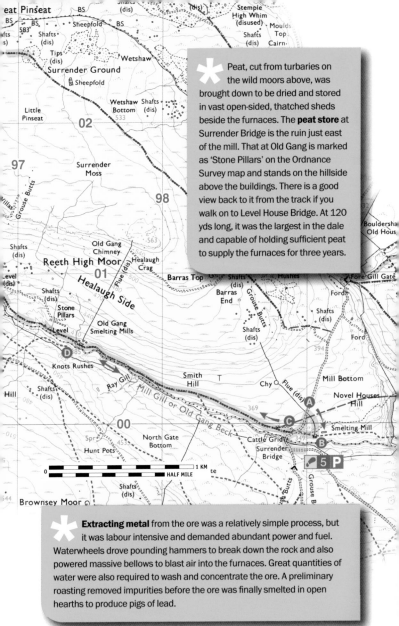

Peat, cut from turbaries on the wild moors above, was brought down to be dried and stored in vast open-sided, thatched sheds beside the furnaces. The **peat store** at Surrender Bridge is the ruin just east of the mill. That at Old Gang is marked as 'Stone Pillars' on the Ordnance Survey map and stands on the hillside above the buildings. There is a good view back to it from the track if you walk on to Level House Bridge. At 120 yds long, it was the largest in the dale and capable of holding sufficient peat to supply the furnaces for three years.

Extracting metal from the ore was a relatively simple process, but it was labour intensive and demanded abundant power and fuel. Waterwheels drove pounding hammers to break down the rock and also powered massive bellows to blast air into the furnaces. Great quantities of water were also required to wash and concentrate the ore. A preliminary roasting removed impurities before the ore was finally smelted in open hearths to produce pigs of lead.

Stainforth to Catrigg Force

■ Wooded gorge   ■ spectacular waterfall
■ far-reaching views   ■ ancient stepping stones

walk 6

A splendid walk over hillsides above the higher Ribble Valley to a dramatic foss on Stainforth Beck, Catrigg Force. From this picturesque spot, where the stream tumbles merrily into an arboreal gully, the return is down an old, stony track that gives grand views towards the distant moors of Bowland to the south west.

Ancient stepping stones at Stainforth

walk 6

START Stainforth

DISTANCE 2$\frac{1}{2}$ miles (4km)

TIME 1$\frac{1}{2}$ hours

PARKING Car park in village (Pay and Display)

ROUTE FEATURES Field paths and tracks; sustained climb at start; *care needed beside waterfall*

GPS WAYPOINTS
- SD 820 672
- Ⓐ SD 826 664
- Ⓑ SD 831 670
- Ⓒ SD 822 674

PUBLIC TRANSPORT Bus service from Settle

REFRESHMENTS Craven Heifer and picnic area in Stainforth

PUBLIC TOILETS Adjoining car park

PLAY AREA None

ORDNANCE SURVEY MAPS Explorer OL2 (Yorkshire Dales – Southern & Western areas), Landranger 98 (Wensleydale & Upper Wharfedale)

Meaning 'stony ford', **Stainforth** takes its name not from Stainforth Beck's stepping stones but from a crossing of the Ribble, which lies just downstream to the west. Although not described in the walk, you can wander down a narrow lane off the main road just north of the village to see Stainforth Bridge, a magnificent parapeted packhorse bridge built in 1670 to replace the ford. You will find another waterfall, a short way below the bridge.

From the car park, turn right into the village and then go right again over a bridge spanning Stainforth Beck. Opposite the Craven Heifer, walk left up a side lane. At the top, turn right and then immediately left onto a track between some cottages, signed to Winskill. Through a gate at the top on the right, walk into a small field, crossing to another gate in its upper corner.

Keep going beside the left-hand fence of a long enclosure until you reach a kissing-gate. From there, a stepped path climbs rather steeply across the wooded bank of Stainforth Scar. Emerging from the trees, go over a stile into a rough field and carry on to a ladder-stile on the far wall. There, bear left towards a farm, Lower Winskill, passing over another stile and through a gate into the yard Ⓐ.

Leave through a gate opposite along a gently rising track to a junction at Upper Winskill. Crossing the farm entrance, keep ahead by the left wall at the edge of open moor. Through a gateway, follow a field track down to a junction and turn left into the next field. Continue dropping to a gate at the bottom corner onto the end of a walled track. A path leaves through a small gate immediately on the right **B** to the gorge and waterfalls of Catrigg Force.

Catrigg Force is one of the prettiest waterfalls in the Dales. The beck drops abruptly in two steps through a narrow cleft in the rock, falling into a deep pool at the head of a wooded gorge, 60 feet below. The fall is variously referred to as 'foss' and 'force', both derivations of the old Norse word fors and a reminder of early settlers in the Dales.

The old lane back to Stainforth

Climb back from the beck to the walled track and turn right, following it down the hill to Stainforth. When you reach the village green **C**, there is a choice of routes back to the car park. You can either bear right between the cottages to ancient stepping stones across the river and then swing left past the church or, alternatively, remain with the lane down to the Craven Heifer and turn right.

> ✱ The **Craven Heifer** is one of several pubs in the district bearing the name. It celebrates a young cow bred in Gargrave at the beginning of the 19th century and which weighed over a ton. The Craven Bank even used its image on a bank note issued in 1817.

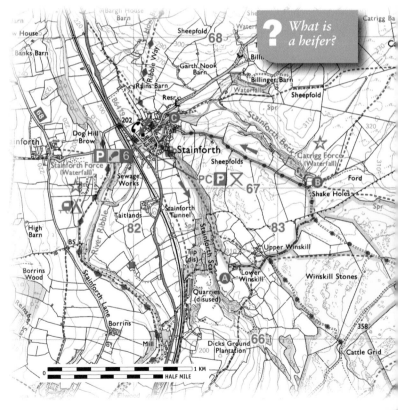

> ❓ *What is a heifer?*

Conistone Pie

- ◼ Dry gorge
- ◼ fine views
- ◼ limestone pavement
- ◼ ancient church

walk 7

A gem of a walk exploring the limestone scenery above Conistone. The climb up a splendid, narrow dry valley is a prelude to a fine upland saunter above the limestone escarpment of Hill Castles. From Conistone Pie – a descriptively distinctive outcrop – there are magnificent views, which linger throughout the return along an old packhorse route.

The view from Conistone Pie

START Conistone

DISTANCE 3 miles (4.8km)

TIME 1½ hours

PARKING Roadside parking by Conistone Bridge

ROUTE FEATURES Field paths and tracks; short and easy scrambles

GPS WAYPOINTS
SD 979 675
Ⓐ SD 992 682
Ⓑ SD 987 686

PUBLIC TRANSPORT Bus services from Skipton

REFRESHMENTS Nearby, Kilnsey Park café and Tennant's Arms

PUBLIC TOILETS None

PLAY AREA None

ORDNANCE SURVEY MAPS Explorer OL2 (Yorkshire Dales – Southern & Western areas), Landranger 98 (Wensleydale & Upper Wharfedale)

The earliest cottages in Wharfedale date from the 17th century, when improvements in agricultural practice brought increasing prosperity and the yeomen farmers began rebuilding their wood and lathe houses and barns in stone. The impressive mullioned windows and carved doorway lintels were an expression of their new confidence.

From Conistone Bridge, walk to a junction in the village centre and bear left. Where the lane then bends left, fork right onto a track, climbing past cottages across an open green. Go through a gate at the top and on between sheep-pens, signposted to Conistone Dib.

What do the numbers on top of the signpost in the village mean?

The way ahead rises into a narrowing gorge that penetrates the high ground behind the village. Once containing a stream, its bed is now dry, and the low steps and falls over which the water once tumbled remain as an easy scramble. At one point so narrow that both sides can be touched at once, the winding valley is full of contrasts, as elsewhere, it widens to hold a green swathe of grazing at its base.

Conistone Dib provides a path onto the hills

Mastiles Lane climbs steeply away up the opposite side of the main valley from the former monastic grange at Kilnsey. Once known as Strete Gate, its origins are perhaps Roman, for it led to a Roman camp near Malham Tarn. Undulating on across the moor, it later formed part of a route connecting Fountains Abbey with its estates in Lakeland and was subsequently used by cattle drovers.

Work your way up the valley, which, towards the top, again narrows, clambering onto a small platform offering a splendid view back to Wharfedale. Just beyond pass through a gate on the right, doubling left above the valley head along a short, walled track to a gate.

Keep ahead, crossing a track, Scot Gate Lane **A** and continue on a level grass path below a low scar. The cliff is, in fact, the edge of an extensive area of limestone pavement. *It is worth making a short detour here to have a look. However, take care in wet or icy weather, for the rocks can become very slippery.* The unmistakable outline of Conistone Pie shortly comes into view, eventually reached over a stile on the left.

After enjoying the view from the top **B**, retrace your steps to the junction with Scot Gate Lane **A**. Turn right to accompany the track down the hillside. After passing a transmitter mast, the way steepens and there are glimpses down into the Dib along which you began the walk. At the bottom, go left along the lane back to the village, passing St Mary's Church.

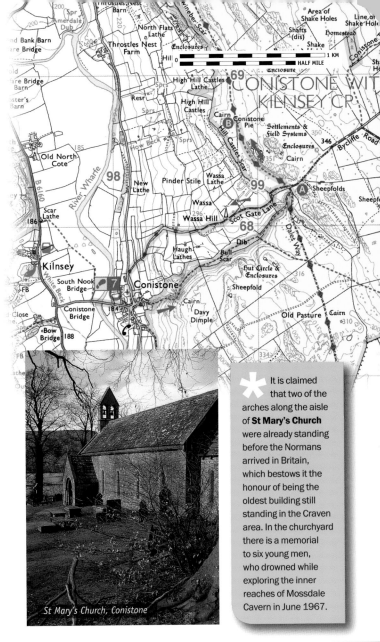

St Mary's Church, Conistone

> ✱ It is claimed that two of the arches along the aisle of **St Mary's Church** were already standing before the Normans arrived in Britain, which bestows it the honour of being the oldest building still standing in the Craven area. In the churchyard there is a memorial to six young men, who drowned while exploring the inner reaches of Mossdale Cavern in June 1967.

Around Burnsall

- Splendid views
- riverside walk
- river cliffs
- historic church

A fine walk from the charming village of Burnsall. After a steep but short climb through well-defined, Anglian field terraces, the route levels across a rolling hillside from where there are stunning views across the valley. The return follows a particularly beautiful section of the Wharfe, which twists unexpectedly below the miniature riverside cliffs of Loup and Wilfrid scars.

The River Wharfe below Loup Scar

walk 8

START Burnsall

DISTANCE 3 miles (4.8km)

TIME 1½ hours

PARKING Car park at edge of village (coin-operated barrier)

ROUTE FEATURES Steep climb along field paths at beginning of walk; narrow suspension bridge

GPS WAYPOINTS
- SE 031 610
- Ⓐ SE 035 614
- Ⓑ SE 037 620
- Ⓒ SE 026 624
- Ⓓ SE 033 616

PUBLIC TRANSPORT Bus services from Ilkley and Skipton

REFRESHMENTS Wharfe View Tea Room and Red Lion in Burnsall

PUBLIC TOILETS Adjoining car park

PLAY AREA None

ORDNANCE SURVEY MAPS Explorer OL2 (Yorkshire Dales – Southern & Western areas), Landranger 98 (Wensleydale & Upper Wharfedale)

Walk towards the village and turn right in front of the Red Lion across the bridge. On the far bank, go left through a gap in the parapet and drop to a field below. Walk upstream to a ladder-stile in the next field and climb steeply up the hillside to a gated squeeze-stile in the top wall Ⓐ.

Cross Skuff Road to the field directly opposite and resume the climb, signposted to Hartlington and Raikes Road. Over a stile at the top, carry on across the next field to a stile in the far wall (not the one tucked into the right-hand corner). Bearing left, walk away on a faint path until, in the third field, you are directed right around the perimeter to a gate opposite South View Farm Ⓑ.

Remain in the field and continue around its edge to cross a stile. Waymarks guide you left, right and then left again along the edges of successive fields. Shortly reaching a gate on the left, gradually move away from the wall, now heading downhill to find a gate, set back

> Burnsall can claim a real-life Dick Whittington in **William Craven**, who in the 16th century, travelled to London to seek his fortune and ended up its Lord Mayor. However, he never forgot his roots and amongst his gifts to the village was a free grammar school. A fine, mullion-windowed building, it still stands beside the church, continuing to serve as the local school.

behind a kink in the bottom wall. Passing through, make for the opposite corner of the field, entering a farmyard at Ranelands.

Walk ahead through the yard to leave through a gate opposite and carry on along the left-hand edge of the field beyond. Ignore a track leaving at the far end, exiting instead over a stile just beyond. Go left past cottages down to a lane and there turn right.

> The 7th-century Bishop of York, St Wilfrid, is credited with founding the chapel here and relics of its ancient past include **Celtic crosses** and **Viking hog-back tombstones**. There is also a beautiful medieval alabaster panel depicting the Adoration. Perhaps the church's most unusual feature is the centrally pivoted **lychgate**, which operates more like a turnstile. Nearby, you will also find the village **stocks**, where miscreants were left to cool their heels for a while.

Some 75 yds beyond Mill Bridge, turn through a small gate into a field on the left **C** and, directed by a 'Dales Way' sign to Burnsall, cross to another gate in the left-hand wall. A narrow suspension bridge takes the route over the Wharfe.

> **?** How old do you think the suspension bridge across the River Wharfe is?

Burnsall from Skuff Road

A clear path follows the riverbank downstream all the way to Burnsall, passing Loup Scar and Wilfrid Scar, where the river runs below small but nevertheless impressive cliffs. Just beyond Wilfrid Scar, you can leave the river beside a cottage **D** to visit Burnsall church. You then have the choice of either continuing down the road through the village or resuming the path by the Wharfe to the bridge. ■

Crossing the River Wharfe

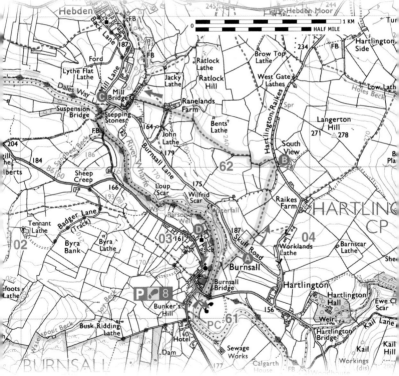

Muker to Ivelet Bridge

- ■ Picturesque village
- ■ Swaledale views
- ■ ancient bridge
- ■ coffin road

walk 9

From the intimacy of winding alleyways and charming stone cottages that is Muker, this walk wanders the valley side giving fine views of upper Swaledale. After dropping to the ancient high-arched packhorse bridge at Ivelet, once a resting point on an ancient corpse way, the route returns by the banks of the lovely River Swale.

An old lane takes the walk out of Muker

walk 9

START Muker

DISTANCE 4¾ miles
(7.6km)

TIME 2½ hours

PARKING Car park
outside village (Pay and
Display)

ROUTE FEATURES Several
short climbs; rough
moorland trod; field
paths

GPS WAYPOINTS
🖉 SD 910 978
Ⓐ SD 921 973
Ⓑ SD 925 972
Ⓒ SD 933 977
Ⓓ SD 915 979
Ⓔ SD 908 987

PUBLIC TRANSPORT Bus
service from Richmond

REFRESHMENTS Tea shop
and inn, the Farmer's
Arms in Muker

PUBLIC TOILETS On main
street in Muker

PLAY AREA None

ORDNANCE SURVEY MAPS
Explorer OL30
(Yorkshire Dales –
Northern & Central
areas), Landranger 98
(Wensleydale & Upper
Wharfedale)

🖉 Leave the car park beside the bridge over
Straw Beck outside Muker, as if to follow the
road to Gunnerside. However, immediately
bear right onto a track, waymarked
'Bridleway and Occupation Road'. After
passing between two barns, the track bends
right to dip across a culverted stream. Just
beyond, go through the second of two gates
on the left.

> ✳ **Sheep farming** has been a mainstay
> of Muker ever since Norsemen
> settled here, but **lead mining** too was once
> important, perhaps begun during the Roman
> occupation of Britain. The industry expanded
> during the 18th and 19th centuries, and
> many of the village's 'new' cottages date
> from this period.

Generally follow the left-hand wall along
the bottom edge of a succession of moorland
enclosures. Eventually emerging through
a gate at Rash, the route continues along
a track. After passing another farmhouse,
drop across a bridge and then turn off
right through a gate to climb towards more
cottages.

Immediately before the cottages, pass through
a narrow gate Ⓐ into a field on the right
and bear left to a wooden stile at the far side.
Climb over and follow the wall up to the left,
crossing more stiles to enter the corner of a
field by a barn. Walk away on a right diagonal

and over another stile at the high point of the top wall. There, turn left through a gate and strike right across a final enclosure to emerge onto a lane **B**.

Go right, but after almost ¼ mile turn off through a waymarked gate on the left. Walk towards the left corner of Kearton's Wood continuing beyond to find a stile in the wall behind. Carry on along the rim of a deepening wooded gully above Oxnop Beck, descending to a farm at Low Oxnop.

Pass the farm to the right and, immediately beyond the barns, negotiate a stile on the left into a field. Carry on above the stream, eventually leaving onto a lane beside Oxnop Bridge. Cross the stream and then turn left down a narrower lane to Ivelet Bridge **C**.

Ivelet Bridge carried a packhorse trail across the River Swale

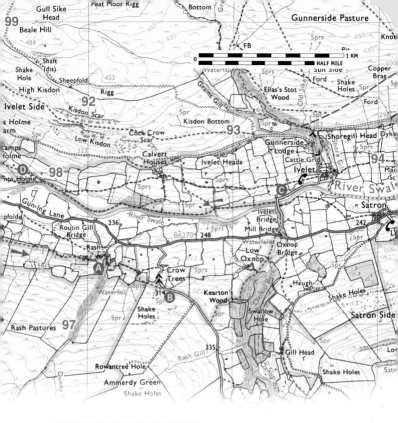

Over the bridge, enter a gate on the left and, for the next mile or so, follow the river upstream towards Muker through a succession of meadows. Eventually, at a gap-stile **D**, a sign to Ramps Holme Bridge directs you away from the Swale, bypassing its confluence with Straw Beck. Carry on beyond Ramps Holme Farm, shortly reaching a fork. Drop to a footbridge across the River Swale.

Above Ramps Holme Bridge

Walking upstream on the opposite bank, ignore a stile on the left from which a paved path crosses the flood meadows direct to Muker. Instead, continue by the river, over a stile and on to a barn. Immediately past it **E**, turn sharp left onto a grass track that rises up the fields behind. Shortly levelling, it carries on through gates as a contained track, in due course meeting a rough lane that descends into Muker. Wind through the village to the main lane and turn left, crossing the bridge back to the car park. ■

St Mary the Virgin is one of the country's few Elizabethan churches and was built as a chapel of ease to save parishioners the long journey to the mother church at Grinton.

? *What was the walled enclosure by the car park in Muker used for?*

Hawes to Hardraw Force

- Famous waterfall
- attractive views
- countryside museum
- rope making

Crossing the Ure's flood meadows onto the valley's northern slopes, this roundabout route to Hardraw offers stunning views across the dale. After visiting the famous waterfall, a spectacular sight especially after heavy rain, there is a leisurely return over the fields to Hawes, where you might visit the Dales Countryside Museum or the nearby rope works.

walk 10

A flagged path leads across the pastures

walk **10**

START Hawes

DISTANCE 4¼ miles (6.8km)

TIME 2 hours

PARKING Car park beside Dales Countryside Museum and National Park Information Centre (Pay and Display)

ROUTE FEATURES Field paths

GPS WAYPOINTS
 SD 875 899
Ⓐ SD 877 905
Ⓑ SD 882 911
Ⓒ SD 867 912

PUBLIC TRANSPORT Bus service from Northallerton

REFRESHMENTS Choice of pubs and cafés in Hawes, Green Dragon Inn and Cart House tearoom at Hardraw

PUBLIC TOILETS Adjoining National Park Information Centre

PLAY AREA Opposite car park

ORDNANCE SURVEY MAPS Explorer OL30 (Yorkshire Dales – Northern & Central areas), Landranger 98 (Wensleydale & Upper Wharfedale)

✱ Located in Hawes' former railway station, the **Dales Countryside Museum** gives an interesting insight into Wensleydale life since its colonisation in the wake of retreating glaciers following the last ice age. Displays illustrate how man's various activities have shaped the character of the dale, with highlights including a reconstructed lead mine and a traditional Dales kitchen.

Start by climbing a path that leaves the car park to the right of the toilets onto Brunt Acres Road. Turn right over a bridge spanning the old railway. After 100 yds swing off towards the town's industrial estate, but immediately leave through a kissing-gate on the right and cut across the fields along a flagged path, rejoining the lane at the far side.

? *Most Yorkshire dales are named after their river, but what is the river here and what gives the dale its name?*

Continue along the lane over the Ure at Haylands Bridge, as far as a stile on the right Ⓐ. A sign directs you diagonally left across the fields towards Sedbusk. Beyond an arched packhorse bridge at the edge of a wood, bear right, gaining height across more fields, and in time, emerging over a stile onto a lane. Cross right to another stile and climb ahead, the route indicated up the fields to Sedbusk.

Beyond a dip, the way rises past a barn to a stile near the top right corner of the last field, leaving onto another lane **B**.

Go right, but then immediately cross a stile on the left and walk to another stile halfway up the left-hand wall. Through that, head away across a succession of narrow fields towards Simonstone, its buildings soon coming into view. Emerging onto a lane, turn left, but then go right along a drive to

> ⁎ The flagged paths radiating from many Dales villages are known as **'causeys'** and were laid to ease the journeys of the coal-miners, lead-miners and quarrymen as they walked to and from their work.

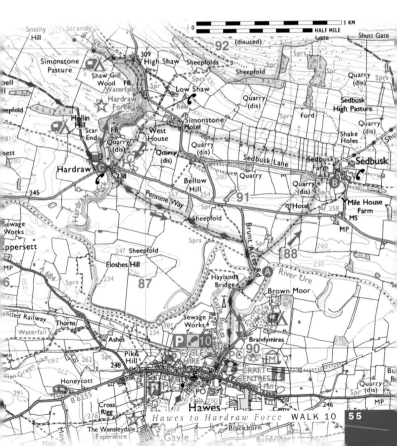

Simonstone Hall Hotel, signposted Hardraw. Just before the cobbled yard, slip through a small gate on the left into a meadow and swing right below the hotel garden to a farm. Go past the farmhouse to a squeeze-stile. Walk left, descending through a couple of fields towards Hardraw and emerging by the Green Dragon Inn .

Packhorse bridge above Hawes

The spectacular falls lie at the head of a narrow gorge, entry to which is through the inn on payment of a small charge. Many of the Victorian visitor paths have been restored and something of the inn's history is revealed in a heritage centre.

The return takes the short track beside the telephone box opposite the inn, signed as the Pennine Way. Through a gate at the end a flagged path leads behind the buildings across the fields.

Rope making has been carried out in Hawes since about 1840, with the Outhwaite factory opening in 1905. Inside you can watch the fascinating process take place, in which fibres are skilfully twisted to produce ropes and cords to suit all manner of purposes.

Keep going where the paved way ends, passing through a gate and continuing above a wall on the right until, finally, you emerge onto Brunt Acres Road. Turn right and retrace your steps to Hawes.

Around Semer Water

- Glacial lake
- erratic boulders
- nature reserve
- abandoned chapel

Fed by rivers rooted in three separate dales, Semer Water owes its existence to a retreating glacier that deposited a moraine across the valley mouth. After following a quiet lane into the valley, the walk crosses the dale to return above the opposite shore, where fields, untouched by modern agricultural practice, have become a haven for plants and wildlife.

walk 11

Semer Water

walk 11

START Semer Water, 2 miles south west of Bainbridge

DISTANCE $3\frac{1}{2}$ miles (5.6km)

TIME $1\frac{1}{2}$ hours

PARKING Car park at foot of lake (charge)

ROUTE FEATURES Narrow stiles; field paths; quiet lane

GPS WAYPOINTS
  SD 922 875
Ⓐ SD 903 862
Ⓑ SD 909 859
Ⓒ SD 916 862

PUBLIC TRANSPORT Bus service to Bainbridge from Leyburn

REFRESHMENTS Nearest at Bainbridge, Corn Mill Tea Room and Rose and Crown

PUBLIC TOILETS Nearest public toilets at Bainbridge

PLAY AREA None

ORDNANCE SURVEY MAPS Explorer OL30 (Yorkshire Dales – Northern & Central areas), Landranger 98 (Wensleydale & Upper Wharfedale)

With the lake on your left, follow the lane from the car park over Semer Water Bridge. Just beyond, turn through a gate on the left into woodland above the shore and, directed by a sign to Marsett Lane, walk ahead. Keep going as the trees thin, joining a wall to find a gate in the corner. Carry on across the next two fields, climbing over a stile in the top fence onto a lane.

Semer Water is all that remains of a huge glacial lake that once filled the valley floor and is one of only two significant natural bodies of water within the Dales, the other being Malham Tarn. The large boulders at the foot of the lake are erratics, brought by the glacier, but are more romantically associated with a battle between the devil and a giant, who hurled them at each other.

To the left, the lane rises gently along the valley, opening delightful views across the lake before you descend to the tiny settlement of Marsett, 1¼ miles away. After crossing Marsett Bridge, go left by a telephone box Ⓐ and then keep left in front of the buildings to follow a track beside Marsett Beck, signed to Semer Water and Stalling Busk.

Shortly, the way diverges from the river to cross the width of the valley. Over Raydale Beck (a footbridge beside the ford gives a dry-shod passage) continue to the next stream, Cragdale Water. There, go over a footbridge Ⓑ into the corner of a rough field and walk

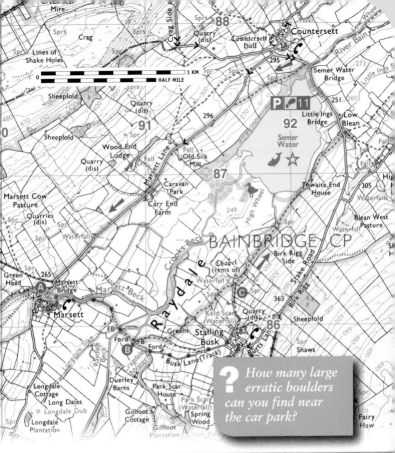

How many large erratic boulders can you find near the car park?

away beside a wall on the right. Cross by a stile 50 yds along and continue up its opposite side.

Keep going to a barn, just past which, turn left through a stile. Walk away, bearing slightly right and maintaining the line across successive fields, gradually gaining

One of the large erratic boulders at Semer Water

The Bain, England's shortest river, begins at Semer Water Bridge

height along the valley side. Eventually, the way is joined by a path from Stalling Busk, just beyond which is a gate into the graveyard of a ruined chapel **C**.

After exploring, return through the gate and go left by the wall into the next field. Continue in the same direction, eventually passing into the Semer Water Nature Reserve.

The path leads through the reserve and, over stiles, continues beside a wall above the lake, shortly leading you into the corner of a pasture by a barn. Walk to a stile on its far side and keep your heading across the subsequent fields.

> ✳ The tiny **church** was founded in 1603 to serve the scattered communities of this lonely dale. Although rebuilt in 1722, it fell into disuse at the beginning of the 20th century after St Matthew's Church was built at nearby Stalling Busk.

Finally emerging over a ladder-stile onto a lane opposite Low Blean Farm, turn left and follow it back down to the car park at the foot of the lake.

Ribblehead Viaduct

- Ribblehead Viaduct
- grand views
- stone-built farms
- disappearing streams

This ramble, which generally follows clear tracks and paths, is one best saved for a fine day to fully enjoy the wild and impressive moorland landscape through which it meanders. Ingleborough and Whernside, the highest of Yorkshire's famous Three Peaks compete for your attention with the Ribblehead Viaduct, a monumental triumph of Victorian engineers.

walk 12

Ribblehead Viaduct

walk 12

START Ribblehead

DISTANCE 4½ miles (7.2km)

TIME 2 hours

PARKING Roadside parking areas at Ribblehead

ROUTE FEATURES Field paths and tracks

GPS WAYPOINTS
- SD 765 792
- Ⓐ SD 757 803
- Ⓑ SD 747 797
- Ⓒ SD 740 791
- Ⓓ SD 747 788
- Ⓔ SD 753 796

PUBLIC TRANSPORT Rail service to Ribblehead

REFRESHMENTS Station Inn

PUBLIC TOILETS None

PLAY AREA None

ORDNANCE SURVEY MAPS Explorer OL2 (Yorkshire Dales – Southern & Western areas), Landranger 98 (Wensleydale & Upper Wharfedale)

Leave the road opposite the B6479 at its junction with the B6255, along a rough trod across the moor towards the viaduct. Join a track going right, but where it later turns beneath the arches, carry on ahead to climb beside the embankment.

> The **Ribblehead Viaduct**, both for its location and scale, is a tribute to all involved in its construction. Twenty-four arches, the highest standing 165 feet above the ground, and two massive embankments carry the track for ¾ mile across the valley head. It is an impressive sight and one of the great feats of Victorian civil engineering.

Keep on until you reach the second accommodation bridge beneath the railway, shortly before the signal-box at Bleamoor Sidings Ⓐ.

Follow a bridleway to cottages at Winterscales, crossing a bridge and later a cattle-grid to reach a junction beyond the farm. Keep ahead, following the track to the next farm, Ivescar, about ⅓ mile away. At a junction by a barn Ⓑ, keep on past the front of the farmhouse, but then bear left through a small yard beside another barn to a field.

Follow a track into a second field, but after crossing a normally dry streambed, curve right to a small gate. Continue in the same direction across more fields to the next farm, Broadrake.

Turn left in front of the farmhouse **C**, and follow a track away. As it later swings right over a cattle-grid, keep ahead through a gate on a

✳ The railway, which runs between Settle and Carlisle, is only the latest in a **succession of routes** that have climbed through the dale to cross the passes into the neighbouring valleys. Throughout the Dales there is a network of prehistoric trods, Roman roads, monastic tracks and packhorse trails, as well as cattle-drove and turnpike roads, many of which are preserved in today's green lanes, footpaths and bridleways.

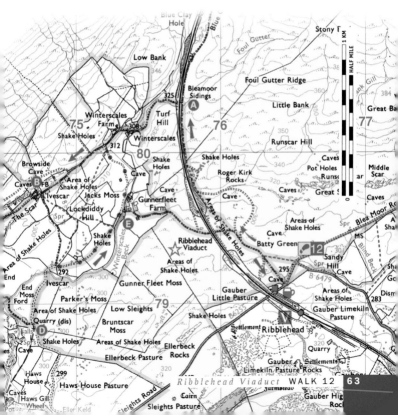

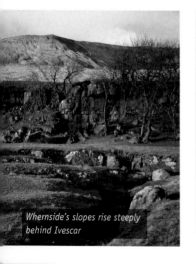

When first encountered near Bleamoor Sidings, **Winterscales Beck** is a boisterous stream, but unless rain has been very heavy, invariably disappears underground in a succession of **sinks** below Gunnerfleet Farm. This, and the equally fascinating phenomenon of stream **resurgence**, is a common feature of the limestone landscape.

Why is the place called Ribblehead?

rough grass track that soon bends left to a ladder-stile. Walk on to cross the (usually) dry bed of Winterscales Beck. Beyond the path curves first right by the streambed and then left parallel to a wall to meet a metalled track **D**.

Walk left and, after recrossing the beck, bear right at a fork. Follow the track through a gate over the fields towards barns at Gunnerfleet Farm and there turn right to cross the stream once more **E**.

Beyond the barns, the track winds towards the viaduct. After passing beneath its towering arches, it leads around to the right, returning you to the road beside the Station Inn back by the starting point. ■

Whernside's slopes rise steeply behind Ivescar

During the construction of the railway, a **shanty town** housing some 2,000 workmen grew up near the viaduct on Batty Moss. The work was hazardous and many men were killed in accidents, but the primitive living conditions in the crude shacks also took their toll, with a smallpox outbreak in 1871 claiming lives among their families too. In all, some 220 people died, three for every mile of track laid. Those that died here lie buried in the pretty little Church of St Leonard's, at nearby Chapel-le-Dale.

Lofthouse to How Stean Gorge

- Pleasant riverside
- Nidderdale views
- hill-top church
- miniature canyon

After a pleasant stroll above the River Nidd, a climb to the tiny village of Middlesmoor is rewarded by one of Nidderdale's finest panoramas from St Chad's churchyard. The onward route lies downhill to How Stean Gorge, where you can break your journey to explore its fascinating natural formations. It is then just a short walk along the lane back to Lofthouse.

walk 13

Looking towards the head of Nidderdale

walk 13

START Lofthouse

DISTANCE 3$\frac{1}{2}$ miles (5.6km)

TIME 1$\frac{1}{2}$ hours

PARKING Car park in village

ROUTE FEATURES Field paths; climb to Middlesmoor

GPS WAYPOINTS

SE 101 734
Ⓐ SE 102 751
Ⓑ SE 095 743
Ⓒ SE 091 741
Ⓓ SE 094 734

PUBLIC TRANSPORT Bus service from Pateley Bridge

REFRESHMENTS Crown Hotels at both Lofthouse and Middlesmoor and café at How Stean Gorge

PUBLIC TOILETS On main road at Lofthouse, by the Crown Hotel at Middlesmoor and at How Stean Gorge for patrons

PLAY AREA How Stean Gorge for patrons

ORDNANCE SURVEY MAPS Explorer OL30 (Yorkshire Dales – Northern & Central areas), Landranger 99 (Northallerton & Ripon)

From the car park, turn right and walk up through Lofthouse. Beyond the top of the village, where the lane bends right onto the open moor, go ahead along a track signed to Scar House Reservoir.

> **?** *Where can you find health advice on the benefits of drinking water?*

> **✳** Although now seemingly miles from anywhere, a **railway** once passed through Lofthouse, laid at the beginning of the 20th century. It carried construction materials to the reservoirs being built at the head of Nidderdale, but also brought passengers as far as Lofthouse. The line closed in 1936, when Scar House, the second of the two dams, was completed.

Following the valley side, the track undulates easily for a mile to reach a small yard at Thrope Farm Ⓐ. Swing left around the farm, dropping behind to a bridge across the River Nidd. On the opposite bank, climb over the left fence and walk away beside the river. Halfway along the field, bear right towards a gate opening in the middle of its end wall, and keep your diagonal across the next field. Leave by a stile towards the far corner of its upper fence onto a lane.

Walk left a few yards to another stile on the right, over which, cut left across the corner to

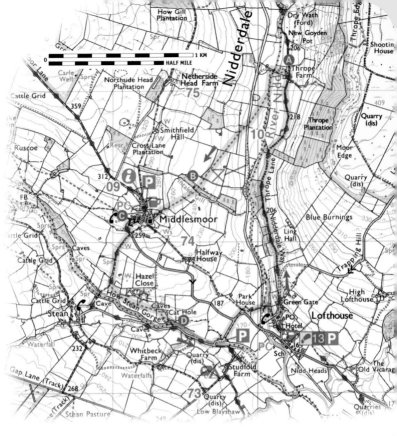

a gap-stile. Head up the adjacent field on a right diagonal to a squeeze-stile in the top wall and continue climbing on the same course across subsequent fields, eventually following a wall towards a stand of conifers **B**.

Pass through the trees and resume your former line, gaining height towards Middlesmoor, which becomes visible ahead. From a final gate, a track leads into the village, passing St Chad's, to meet the main street **C**, just below the Crown Hotel.

Turn left down the hill and out of the village. Just after a sharp left-hand bend, cross a stile beside a gate into the field on the right and follow its boundary away from the road. Continue down the next two fields until you reach a squeeze-stile in the wall on the right. Instead of going through, swing left and cross to the right-hand of two gates in the far wall.

Keep going over subsequent fields to pass through a gate, just right of a barn. Turn right through a second gate into a field above How Stean Gorge. The entrance (admission charge) and café lie over a bridge at the bottom, spanning the miniature canyon.

Walk out onto the lane ⓓ and go left, following it above the gorge to a junction. Turn left over a bridge and then right at a second junction. Leave on a sharp bend through a kissing-gate ahead, bearing right and then left beside the cricket green to emerge opposite the fire station. Cross to a bridge beside it and follow the ensuing path into the village. The car park and Crown Hotel are just to the right. ■

Across Nidderdale to Middlesmoor

Kirkby Malham to Airton

- Attractive villages
- riverside meadows
- Pennine Way
- interesting church

From Kirkby Malham, whose church has been described as the 'Cathedral of the Dales', this walk wanders across infrequently traversed green pastures to the peaceful hamlet of Airton. Of interest there is a Quaker Meeting House, squatter's cottage and one-time mill. The return allows a leisurely amble along meadows beside the meandering River Aire.

walk 14

The path beside the River Aire

walk 14

START Kirkby Malham

DISTANCE 3¾ miles (6km)

TIME 2 hours

PARKING Parking area by the church

ROUTE FEATURES Field paths and trods

GPS WAYPOINTS

 SD 893 609
Ⓐ SD 889 602
Ⓑ SD 900 595
Ⓒ SD 904 592
Ⓓ SD 899 611

PUBLIC TRANSPORT Bus service from Skipton

REFRESHMENTS Victoria pub at Kirkby Malham, Town End Farm tearoom at Airton

PUBLIC TOILETS Nearest are at Malham

PLAY AREA None

ORDNANCE SURVEY MAPS Explorer OL2 (Yorkshire Dales – Southern & Western areas), Landrangers 98 (Wensleydale & Upper Wharfedale) and 103 (Blackburn & Burnley)

From the parking area opposite St Michael's Church, a path, signed to Otterburn, dips across Kirkby Beck before rising to a field above the gorge. Cut to a stile on the right and then, bearing slightly left, head towards another stile at the top corner below a wood. Climb beside the trees.

Reaching a track, cross to the field opposite and strike a left diagonal to its far corner. Cross a small bridge to a stile and follow the left wall up 100 yds to a gate Ⓐ. Walk across the field, a developing track leading through a gate to a barn beyond its far tip.

Turn right in front of the barn through a wayposted gate. Head for a stile in the distant left corner and maintain the line across successive fields for a good ¼ mile, eventually curving right towards large barns at Moor End Farm.

Ignoring the fence-stile just before the barns, turn left across the field, following overhead

Hanlith Bridge across the River Aire

power cables. Then, over a stone stile carry on beside a wall on the left until you reach a stile just short of the corner **B**. There, turn right, crossing to a ladder-stile on the far wall and continue over the remaining fields to emerge onto a lane among the cottages of Airton.

Britain's first long-distance footpath, the **Pennine Way**, was opened in 1965 and runs for 270 miles from Edale in Derbyshire to Kirk Yetholm in the Cheviots. The stretch on this walk is a pleasing contrast to much of its route, which more generally lies across exposed and desolate moorland.

At a junction just to the right, turn sharp left and then immediately right onto a track, signposted Town End, which leaves the road between the drives of two houses. Follow it behind the village to another lane. There go left and walk down to the main road.

Carry on straight over towards Calton beside the village green. Just across a bridge over the River Aire **C**, double back left and go over a stile into a meadow by the river, signposted Pennine Way. The route picks its way along the riverside pastures for nearly ½ mile before moving away from the water to find a gate and footbridge spanning Crook Syke.

Cross and go right, signed to Hanlith, shortly rejoining the River Aire farther upstream. After a mile, a final stile leads onto a lane near Hanlith Hall **D**. Turn left, cross the Aire and walk up the lane for ½ mile back to Kirkby Malham. ∎

Kirkby Malham

? What is carved under the niche on the middle pillar of the south aisle of St Michael's Church?

Grassington to Grass Wood

- ◼ Lively village
- ◼ folk museum
- ◼ woodland nature reserve
- ◼ riverside walk

Characterful Grassington makes an interesting start for this enjoyable saunter to Grass Wood. One of many sites of local prehistoric settlement, the woodland sustains a rich variety of animal and plant life and is particularly beautiful in spring and early summer. The circuit is completed by a relaxing amble along an attractive stretch of the River Wharfe.

walk 15

Main Street through Grassington

walk 15

START National Park Information Centre outside Grassington

DISTANCE 5 miles (8km)

TIME 2½ hours

PARKING Car park beside Information Centre (Pay and Display)

ROUTE FEATURES Generally clear paths and tracks

GPS WAYPOINTS
 SE 003 637
Ⓐ SE 003 642
Ⓑ SE 002 646
Ⓒ SD 995 650
Ⓓ SD 981 657
Ⓔ SD 982 652
Ⓕ SD 998 638

PUBLIC TRANSPORT Bus service from Skipton

REFRESHMENTS Café within Information Centre and a choice of cafés and pubs in Grassington

PUBLIC TOILETS Adjoining car park

PLAY AREA None

ORDNANCE SURVEY MAPS Explorer OL2 (Yorkshire Dales – Southern & Western areas), Landranger 98 (Wensleydale & Upper Wharfedale)

Go left from the car park towards Grassington and, at the village, turn right into Main Street.

> At the bottom of Grassington, overlooking the square, two former **miners' cottages** house a fascinating museum, which gives an insight into the life, industry and natural history of the dale.

Climb past the shops to the top of the town and bear left by the Devonshire Institute Ⓐ into Chapel Street towards Town Head. After 275 yds, turn right onto a track, Bank Lane. Picking up signs for Dales Way and Grass Wood Lane, walk up to a fork and go through a hand-gate on the left Ⓑ.

Stride out across a field to a stile, and then, following signs, head left to another stile. Cross a track from the farm to a wall-stile opposite and strike a right diagonal across a sloping field towards distant Grass Wood. A stile at the far corner leads out onto the corner of a walled track.

Walk ahead past barns to the end of the track and pass through the right-hand one of the two gates. Keep going along a narrow field and then bear right across the next enclosure to a stone stile into Grass Wood Ⓒ.

Ignore side tracks as you follow a twisting trail. It climbs through the trees and eventually levels as a surfaced path. At a crossing of paths, remain ahead, directed by a sign towards Grass Wood Lane. However, at a waymark a little farther on, turn off right onto a narrower grass path. Keep going as it descends, later swinging sharply left and running on to rejoin the gravel way.

Once the site of an Iron Age encampment, and more recently exploited for its timber, **Grass Wood** is now managed to benefit local native varieties of both tree and plant life. The diversity of species makes it a delight, particularly in spring when woodland birds and flowers make their appearance.

Ghaistrill's Strid, above Grassington

Just before a gate out of the wood
D, turn left onto an unsurfaced
path climbing above Grass Wood
Lane. After cresting the rise, a path
joins from the left. Carry on for
another 20 yds to find a lesser path
leaving on the right, which drops back to
the lane. Go through a gate opposite **E**
into the lower half of the wood.

A path between the trees signed to Grassington
leads to the River Wharfe, where it continues
downstream. Later leaving the wood, the way
remains by the riverbank, passing through a succession
of waterside meadows. Approaching a bridge, bear left
over the final field and climb to the road **F**.

Cross to a gate in the opposite wall, through which a path signed
to Hebden and Burnsall drops back to the riverside meadows. Keep
going downstream until you reach a footbridge bringing a path across

the river from Linton. Now turn left
onto a walled, paved path, Sedber
Lane, and follow it up the hill back
to the car park from which the
walk began.   ■

At the edge of Grass Wood

> ✻ Native Britons once farmed
> the surrounding hills and,
> although not easily identifiable to
> the untrained eye, the slopes above
> Grassington are littered with remains
> of **Iron Age settlements** and field
> systems. Throughout the medieval
> period the town remained an
> important centre and was granted a
> market charter as early as 1282.

? **What were the weirs straddling the river downstream of Grassington for?**

The arrival of the turnpike in the 18th century, the development of lead mining on the moors and the conversion of local corn mills for the textile industry brought a new wealth to **Grassington**. The boom continued until foreign imports slashed the price of lead and the introduction of steam power left the water-driven textile mills unable to compete. However, the local economy found a new boost in the arrival of the railway in 1901, which heralded the birth of a tourist industry.

Wharfedale, Barden Tower and The Strid

■ Beautiful woods   ■ Barden Tower

■ lovely riverside   ■ The Strid

walk 16

This is a popular ramble revealing the charm of Wharfedale. Spectacular viewpoints punctuate the undulating upstream woodland walk, which culminates at Barden Tower, a medieval forest lodge. Returning beside the river, the walk winds through Strid Wood, which is noted for its wealth of plants and wildlife and is especially enchanting in spring and early summer.

The ruins of Barden Tower, a medieval hunting lodge

walk 16

Cross the River Wharfe by the footbridge opposite the Cavendish Pavilion and Information Centre and then immediately turn left to follow a path upstream on the opposite bank. Farther on, through a gate, take the stepped path, but keep left to remain by the river. Beyond Ludstream Islands the path curves towards the lane beside Posforth Bridge Ⓐ.

After crossing Posforth Gill footbridge, wind back through the trees. Farther upstream, the path climbs high above the river, passing a shelter from which there is a magnificent view back along the valley.

Beyond, the path remains elevated above The Strid, giving a dramatic perspective over the river's constriction through a narrow cleft in the bedrock. You will get an opportunity to see it at close quarters on the way back. As you progress, occasional benches beside the path mark some of the most spectacular viewpoints along the valley.

Shortly, the way falls, eventually leaving the wood and rejoining the riverbank by a stone bridge Ⓑ. This is actually an aqueduct, which carries water from Grimwith Reservoir over the river.

To shorten the walk, you could cross the river here to join the return route, but you would then miss Barden Tower, which lies about ½ mile farther on. Continue on this bank along riverside meadows, finally emerging onto a lane beside the next bridge upstream. Go over the Wharfe and walk up the hill until you reach a stile on the left. Barden Tower rises impressively at the top of the field **C**.

Return towards the bridge but, just before it, leave the road through a small gate on the right and follow a path on the river's western bank back downstream. In a little while, beyond the aqueduct, a footbridge takes the route over a side stream into Strid Wood.

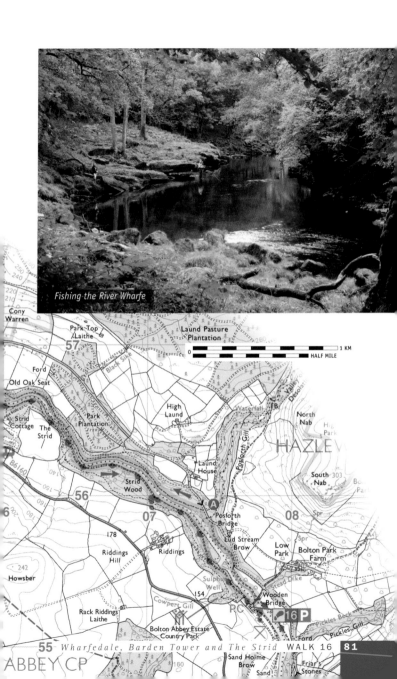

Fishing the River Wharfe

The Strid

Although barely 6 feet wide at its narrowest, the underwater chasm is some 30 feet deep, and the roaring torrent has claimed many a life from those foolhardy enough to attempt the leap across **The Strid**. Legend has it that a son of the de Romilles, Norman founders of Skipton Castle, lost his life there during a hunting expedition. In his memory, his mother gave land by the Wharfe to Augustinian canons, on which they founded nearby Bolton Priory.

Ignore tracks off to the right and, after rising past a viewpoint, choose the lower branch at a fork for the best views of the river. At another split farther on, again bear left to drop to a large, rocky platform by the water at The Strid.

Downstream, the path later divides, that to the left remaining by the riverbank to end at Ludstream Islands where a hide overlooks the water. The way back, however, is along the main path, which takes a higher line across the wooded slope above the islands back to the Pavilion. ■

The River Wharfe below Barden Bridge

How many different types of trees and wild flowers can you find in the woods? (Remember that it is illegal to pick wild flowers.)

Reeth to Marrick Abbey

■ Folk museum   ■ site of abbey

■ valley views   ■ ancient earthworks

From Reeth, above the confluence of the Arkle and Swale, hillside pastures open wonderful views along the valley. An idyllic woodland pathway leads on to the former nunnery at Marrick and the return is an easy ramble above the River Swale. Call at St Andrew's in Grinton, the 'mother church' of Swaledale, or visit Reeth's fascinating museum of Swaledale life.

walk 17

The riverside path follows the Swale to Grinton

walk 17

START Reeth

DISTANCE 6 miles (9.7km)

TIME 3 hours

PARKING Car park above village and around the green (honesty box)

ROUTE FEATURES Sustained climb along quiet lane; field paths and tracks

GPS WAYPOINTS
- 🔳 SE 038 993
- Ⓐ SE 046 991
- Ⓑ SE 065 987
- Ⓒ SE 076 981
- Ⓓ SE 066 978
- Ⓔ SE 054 986
- Ⓕ SE 046 985

PUBLIC TRANSPORT Bus service from Richmond

REFRESHMENTS Choice of pubs and tearooms in Reeth, and the Bridge Inn at Grinton

PUBLIC TOILETS Overlooking village green at Reeth

PLAY AREA None

ORDNANCE SURVEY MAPS Explorer OL30 (Yorkshire Dales – Northern & Central areas), Landrangers 98 (Wensleydale & Upper Wharfedale) and 99 (Northallerton & Ripon)

🥾 Leave the top of the village green by Ivy Cottage Tea Room, passing the Arkleside Country Guest House before dropping to the right. Keep ahead at the bottom, by Arkle House, and then turn right onto a path beside Arkle Beck. Passing beneath a bridge, turn up to the road and cross the river.

✴ There are numerous **earthworks** around Reeth, some dating from the Bronze Age. However, the impressive mounds beside the river around Grinton are part of defences thrown up around AD70 by native Britons, attempting to stay the advance of Roman invaders.

Bend in front of a car-sales forecourt, and immediately go left through a waymarked gate. Bear right across the corner into the adjacent field and carry on in the same direction to a small gate, partway along the

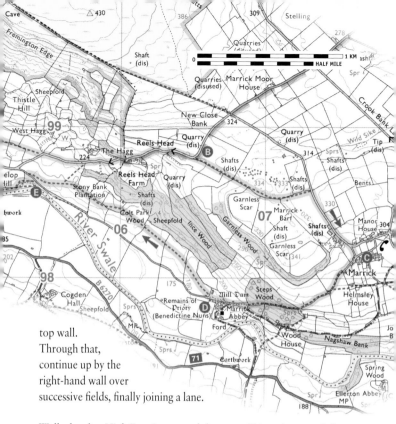

top wall.
Through that,
continue up by the
right-hand wall over
successive fields, finally joining a lane.

Walk ahead to High Fremington and there, at a T-junction, turn left to climb in front of a cottage. Just beyond, take a walled footpath beside it **Ⓐ**, but where that bends behind the cottage, go forward through a stile into the corner of a field. Carry on across the fields to emerge over a final stile onto a lane.

The climb to the left through a wood is quite steep, but eventually levels beyond Reels Head, where the lane bends sharply left. There, at a fingerpost **Ⓑ**, go through the second of two gates on the right and walk away beside the right-hand wall.

Carry on across the fields until, after passing beneath a power line, you reach a stile on the right. Cross and continue down on the opposite side

The Nun's Causeway through Steps Wood

of the wall. A final stile leads onto a lane, where you should turn right.

The descent towards Marrick offers splendid views across Swaledale. As the lane bends left into the village above a small green, bear right down to a farm and turn right again **C**.

Follow the track to its end and walk on through a gate down the ensuing fields, keeping ahead partway down through a small yard by a barn. In Steps Wood, an old flagged path maintains the steady descent, dropping out through a field onto a metalled track at the bottom. Go right past Marrick Abbey.

> The 12th century saw the founding of many religious houses in the area. Not a mile apart, two separate nunneries were established; one downstream at Ellerton under the Cistercians and here at Marrick by the Benedictine order. Although the sisters were expelled at the Dissolution, the church was still used by the village and the pretty woodland path, known as the **Nun's Causeway**, was paved as the route between the two.

You could simply follow the track for the next mile. However, for better views, as you leave the farm, bear right below an abandoned corrugated hut through a gate **D**. Walk across the middle of this and the next two fields. Then, over a ladder-stile, follow a fence and subsequent wall on your left, eventually crossing it over a squeeze-stile.

Walk away, keeping the same direction across the remaining fields, finally entering a larger field. Towards its far end, bear left to rejoin the track from Marrick Abbey over a stile. Turn left and walk back 50 yds to

? *Why are there so many large inns at Reeth?*

Housed in the former Methodist schoolroom, the **Swaledale Folk Museum** depicts many aspects of Dales life, showing the impact which local industries, such as agriculture, mining and knitting, have had upon social conditions.

a stile on the right **E**. A path follows the Swale for ½ mile upstream to Grinton Bridge.

Cross the road to a gap diagonally opposite **F**, from which a faint path gently curves across the fields to a farm by Arkle Beck. Continue upstream to the road and follow it back over Reeth Bridge. You can then either retrace your outward steps beside the river or continue up the road into the village back to the starting point.

The path out of Reeth

Buckden to Hubberholme

- Excellent views
- limestone scenery
- ancient church
- stepping stones

walk 18

This lovely walk explores the terraced limestone countryside of Upper Wharfedale. The ascent of Buckden Rake and traverse above Cray Gill and Hubberholme are rewarded by superb views along the wide, flat-bottomed valley. After passing the lovely old church at Hubberholme, the route concludes with a gentle riverside stroll.

The terraces of Buckden Moor above Cray Gill

walk 18

START Buckden

DISTANCE 5 miles (8km)

TIME 2½ hours

PARKING Car park in village (Pay and Display)

ROUTE FEATURES Sustained climb; field paths; stepping stones

GPS WAYPOINTS
- SD 942 773
- Ⓐ SD 942 791
- Ⓑ SD 921 789
- Ⓒ SD 926 782

PUBLIC TRANSPORT Bus service from Skipton

REFRESHMENTS Café and Buck Inn in Buckden, White Lion Inn at Cray, George Inn at Hubberholme

PUBLIC TOILETS Adjoining car park

PLAY AREA None

ORDNANCE SURVEY MAPS OL30 (Yorkshire Dales – Northern & Central areas), Landranger 98 (Wensleydale & Upper Wharfedale)

✳ Buckden was the administrative centre of the Percy's great **hunting forest** of Langstrothdale. Forest laws were enforced and the feudal court presided to set fines and punish infringements such as poaching. Later, when the monastic estates developed the hillsides into vast sheep runs, the village evolved as an important market for the wool.

🖉 A track leaves through a gate from the northern end of the car park, signposted Cray High Bridge and Buckden Pike. It steadily rises through Buckden Wood along the steep valley side above the road to Bishopdale. Beyond the trees, the way continues through gates at the edge of upland pastures. Shortly levelling off, it discretely turns its back on Wharfedale and heads into a side valley that holds Cray Gill at its base.

Ignore a path later leaving on the right to Buckden Pike and keep ahead towards Cray High Bridge. However, ⅓ mile farther on, go through a small gate in the wall on the left, signposted Cray. A path, initially quite steep, picks its way down the terraced hillside to a gate at the bottom right-hand corner of the enclosure. Stepping stones take the route across the river onto a lane opposite the White Lion Ⓐ.

Directly opposite, a track leads behind the inn signed to Stubbing Bridge and Yockenthwaite. Bear right up to a barn and go forward

Limestone terraces above Todd's Wood

through a gated yard. The path leads past more buildings, soon reaching a signpost. Keep straight on passing through a gate towards Scar House and Yockenthwaite.

The way continues ahead through a succession of enclosures, shortly leading over a footbridge above a stream, Crook Gill. On the far bank, go left following a fence line above the steep slopes of Todd's Wood. A mile of easy walking eventually brings you to a junction above Scar House **B**.

Turn left onto a track, signposted Hubberholme, which drops past the house and descends along the side of the valley. After joining the Dales Way at the bottom, the route winds around Hubberholme church before leading out onto a minor lane at the end. Turn past the entrance to the churchyard and cross a bridge over the River Wharfe to a junction in front of the George Inn **C**.

? *How did Buckden get its name?*

Follow the lane to the left for almost ½ mile, where you can then leave through a gate on the left. A path, signposted to Buckden Bridge follows the field perimeter down to the Wharfe before winding pleasantly beside the river towards Buckden. When you get to the final field, before reaching a bridge, cut across to return to the lane. Follow it over the River Wharfe to get back to the starting point in the village. ■

The teachings of George Fox found a chord in the independence of the Dales people, and his ideas that became **Quakerism** flourished amongst these isolated settlements. Despite the persecution that was visited on members of the sect, James Tennant of Scar House welcomed Fox to his home in 1652 and 1677. However, his support for the movement landed him in prison at York, where he subsequently died for his beliefs.

Crossing Cray Gill

Settle to Victoria and Jubilee Caves

- ▩ **Wild moorland**
- ▩ **caves**
- ▩ **geological fault**
- ▩ **interesting town**

Above the cliffs, once perceived to threaten the town with destruction, a wild, moorland landscape is backed by the stark, dramatic crags of Attermire Scar. After traversing its base, a gentle descent above the Ribble gives ample opportunity to enjoy some fine views and, back in Settle, you might end the day with an exploration of the town and a visit to its museum.

walk 19

Fine views across the Ribble Valley on the return section

walk **19**

START Settle

DISTANCE 5¼ miles (8.4km)

TIME 3 hours

PARKING Greenfoot car park (Pay and Display)

ROUTE FEATURES Sustained climb; tracks and field paths

GPS WAYPOINTS
- 🔲 SD 820 634
- Ⓐ SD 833 627
- Ⓑ SD 838 640
- Ⓒ SD 838 650
- Ⓓ SD 837 655
- Ⓔ SD 829 653

PUBLIC TRANSPORT Bus and rail services from Skipton

REFRESHMENTS Choice of cafés and pubs in Settle, picnic area above Upper Settle

PUBLIC TOILETS In Settle's market square

PLAY AREA Above car park at start of walk

ORDNANCE SURVEY MAPS Explorer OL2 (Yorkshire Dales – Southern & Western areas), Landranger 98 (Wensleydale & Upper Wharfedale)

✱ With many fine buildings, some dating to the 17th century, **Settle** is an attractive, bustling market town. **The Shambles**, in the market square, was originally an open market, the arcading and an upper storey being added later. One of the houses overlooking the square was the home of Dr Buck, to which his friend the composer Edward Elgar often came to stay. Nearby is **Tanner Hall**, with its fine, mullioned façade, built by a local tanner, Richard Preston. He supposedly spent more than he could afford on the building and it became known as Richard's Folly.

? *Look for a strange sign on Ye Old Naked Man café, opposite the Market Square in Settle. What does it mean?*

🥾 A path climbs the lawned bank behind the car park onto Commercial Street. Go left to a junction and then right up Albert Hill, signed to Kirkby Malham and Airton. Where the street forks, continue ahead along Greenhead Lane and, beyond some cottages, bear left before a small picnic area on the site of the old pinfold or cattle pound onto a gravel track, marked to Lambert Lane.

At the top of a steep climb by the entrance to Settle High Reservoir, cross a stile and climb by the left wall, swinging within the corner to reach a gap-stile. Head up the adjacent field to a ladder-stile. Over that follow the wall on your left around the perimeter. Cross a stile into the next field and eventually leave through a gate onto a walled track, Lambert Lane .

Go left to a lane at its end and turn right. Then, at a bend 100 yds on, bear left along a metalled track, Stockdale Lane, signed as the Pennine

High cliffs, or scars, mark the line of the Craven Fault

Bridleway. After 200 yds, at a sharp right-hand turn, go ahead over a ladder-stile and up a gravel track, waymarked to Attermire Scar. Over the crest, where the gravel ends, continue on a green path, passing left of Sugar Loaf Hill.

Curving right beyond the grassy hillock, follow a wall, making for a stile to the right of a gate below Warrendale Knotts **B**.

Turn right past a curious mound, the remains of the Attermire Rifle Range target, then swing left to climb through a break in the higher ground. Reaching a ladder-stile, cross the wall and continue up on its other flank.

The gradient soon eases and the path follows the base of the scree below the cliff. After passing through a kissing-gate carry on below Victoria Cave. You can climb to its mouth **C**, from which there is a superb view back across the valley, *but are advised not to enter because of the danger of rock falls.* Continue to a second gate at the northern end of the scar, beyond which the path drops to a track.

As the last ice age retreated, small groups of people began to settle the hill slopes, often choosing caves as convenient shelters. Excavations in **Victoria Cave**, so named for its discovery in the year of the Queen's coronation, have revealed flints and bone tools, as well as the remains of several species of animals. There was also evidence that the caves were used during the Roman period, perhaps by bands of native Britons hiding from the invading forces.

Turn right and walk up to Jubilee Cave **D**, which again lies to the right of the track, some 200 yds along.

After exploring, go back to the track, crossing to a ladder-stile diagonally opposite. Walk directly away from the wall, keeping ahead over a crossing to follow a gently descending faint path across the open hillside. Meeting a gravel track at the far end, go right over a cattle-grid onto a lane **E**.

Through a gate on the left, a green path is signed to Settle. After following a wall at the edge of a wood, carry on to cross through a second stand of trees in front. The way continues in the same direction over successive fields, falling towards the town, which before long appears ahead.

Jubilee Cave

Eventually developing as a track and subsequently a lane, the route descends Constitution Hill into Settle. Go left at a junction onto Castle Hill, but then fork right along a paved street towards the centre of town. To return to the car park, walk left along High Street and keep straight over the next junction near The Folly, which houses the Museum of North Craven Life, back to Greenfoot car park. ■

Malham Cove, Gordale Scar & Janet's Foss

■ **Stunning scenery**   ■ **dry valley**
■ **stream resurgence**   ■ **waterfalls**

walk 20

This popular walk offers spectacular scenery, with breathtaking views above Malham Cove's huge amphitheatre a sharp contrast to the dark confines of Gordale, where a lusty waterfall cascades into the gorge. Lower down, it is the same stream that tumbles picturesquely over Janet's Foss, from which a delightful return stroll beckons through woodland and meadows.

The dramatic walk into Gordale

START Malham

DISTANCE 5 miles (8km)

TIME 2½ hours

PARKING Car park south of village (Pay and Display)

ROUTE FEATURES Field paths; steep, stepped path; *unguarded cliffs and slippery rocks*

GPS WAYPOINTS

📍 SD 900 626
🅐 SD 898 632
🅑 SD 897 640
🅒 SD 897 641
🅓 SD 902 637
🅔 SD 915 640
🅕 SD 902 624

PUBLIC TRANSPORT Bus service from Skipton

REFRESHMENTS Several cafés and two pubs, Listers Arms Hotel and Buck Inn in Malham

PUBLIC TOILETS Adjoining car park and beside Buck Inn

PLAY AREA None

ORDNANCE SURVEY MAPS Explorer OL2 (Yorkshire Dales – Southern & Western areas), Landranger 98 (Wensleydale & Upper Wharfedale)

From the car park, turn left through the village, going ahead at the junction just past the Buck Inn. After ⅓ mile, just beyond the National Trust-owned Town Head Barn, go through a gate on the right, signed as the Pennine Way 🅐. An undulating path briefly parallels the lane before heading up the valley to the foot of Malham Cove, whose massive amphitheatre dominates the head of the landscape.

Having explored the base of the cove, walk back a short way and fork right 🅑 to climb a steep, but well-laid, stepped path to the top

⁕ The massive amphitheatre of **Malham Cove** is the finest limestone cirque in Britain, rising vertically over 250 feet above its base and extending 1,000 feet around the head of the valley. It is part of the Craven Fault system, which is revealed in the lines of sheer scars that dominate the area. At one time a waterfall cascaded over its lip, fed by Malham Tarn, 1¼ miles to the north. The water now falls into a sink, just south of the lake, leaving a fine example of a **dry valley** running to the top of the cove. The **river** that reappears at its base, however, is actually from a different source, a stream rising on the moor to the west of the tarn. Malham Tarn's waters, the source of the River Aire, resurge at Aire Head, just south of Malham.

of the cliff. Carefully pick your way to the right over the expanse of limestone pavement above the head of the cove to a wall at its far

Clapper bridge across Malham Beck

side. Cross it by a ladder-stile **C**, just a little way back from the cliff edge.

Walk away, curving right up a gently rising hillside. At a fingerpost, join another path from the left to follow a stretch of wall. Continue across an undulating, rock-scarred landscape before finally emerging over a stile onto a lane **D**.

Janet was a **fairy queen**, who lived in the cave beside the foss. Apart from being a delightful waterfall, it is interesting because of its **tufa** formation. Evaporating water, collecting on mosses around the lip of the fall, leaves behind a residue of fragile limestone, a process similar to that responsible for many formations in caves.

Cross to a kissing-gate, from which a clear path is signed to Gordale. After contouring the rising ground, the way passes through a small enclosure at the base of a scree-filled gully. Beyond there, through a gate on the right, walk diagonally across the field below to another gate, then follow the wall on your left down, finally emerging onto a lane by a bridge over Gordale Beck.

Head left up the lane to
a bend and there leave through
a gate on the left. A path across a camping
meadow beside the beck leads into a gorge below
Gordale Scar, taking you to the foot of a waterfall at its head **E**.

Walk back down the gorge to the lane and turn right, continuing past
the bridge met earlier. Just beyond the wall of a ruined barn, 100 yds
farther on, go through a gate on the left, from which a riverside path
is signed to Malham. Almost immediately, to the left of the path, is a

vantage above Janet's Foss, the main route dropping to a pool at its base.

? *What was the pool below Janet's Foss used for?*

The way progresses beside the beck through a pretty wooded gorge. Keep going across the valley bottom, to the meadows beyond, in time passing the end of a walled track. Reaching a junction, just beyond a barn **F**, go right through a gate. The path soon joins Malham Beck back to the village. ■

The waterfall at the head of Gordale

Further Information

Walking safety

The uplands and moors of Britain, though of modest height compared with those in many other countries, need to be treated with respect. Friendly and inviting when the sun shines, they can quickly become transformed into wet, misty, windswept and potentially dangerous areas of wilderness in bad weather. Even on an apparently fine and settled summer day, conditions can rapidly deteriorate. In winter, of course, the weather can be even more erratic and the hours of daylight are much shorter.

Therefore it is advisable always to take both warm and waterproof clothing, sufficient nourishing food, a hot drink, first-aid kit, torch

Malham Cove

Repairing a drystone wall

Follow the Country Code

- Be safe, plan ahead and follow any signs
- Leave gates and property as you find them
- Protect plants and animals and take your litter home
- Keep dogs under close control
- Consider other people

(Natural England)

and whistle. Wear suitable footwear such as strong walking boots or shoes that give a good grip over rocky terrain and on slippery slopes. A few simple rules will help ensure your safety: have regard to the local weather forecast, do not be afraid to abandon your proposed route in the event of a sudden and unexpected deterioration in the weather or the walk is more demanding than you anticipated, do not go alone and allow enough time to finish the walk well before nightfall.

The walks described in this book do not venture far into remote wilderness areas and should be safe to do, given due care and reasonable weather, at any time of year. Indeed, a crisp, fine winter's day often provides perfect walking conditions, with firm ground underfoot and an atmospheric clarity that is rarely present in other seasons. You should, however, be appropriately fit and experienced for the length and terrain of the walk and able to use a map and compass. If you have a dog, be aware of its limitations too, particularly with regard to stiles.

Useful Organisations

Campaign to Protect Rural England
128 Southwark Street,
London SE1 0SW
Tel. 020 7981 2800
www.cpre.org.uk

Campaign for National Parks
6/7 Barnard Mews, London
SW11 1QU
Tel. 020 7924 4077
www.cnp.org.uk

English Heritage
1 Waterhouse Square, 138 – 142
Holborn, London EC1N 2ST
Tel. 0870 333 1181
www.english-heritage.org.uk
Yorkshire Regional Office
Tel. 01904 601 901

National Trust
Membership and general enquiries:
PO Box 39, Warrington WA5 7WD
Tel. 0844 800 1895
www.nationaltrust.org.uk
Yorkshire Regional Office:
Goddards, 27 Tadcaster Road,
Dringhouses, York YO24 1GG
Tel. 01904 702021

Natural England
1 East Parade, Sheffield S1 2ET
Tel. 0845 600 3078
www.naturalengland.org.uk

Ordnance Survey
Tel. 08456 05 05 05 (Lo-call)
www.ordnancesurvey.co.uk

Traveline
www.traveline.org.uk
Tel. 0871 200 22 33

Traveldales
Tel. 0300 456 00 30
www.traveldales.org.uk

Ramblers
2nd Floor, Camelford House,
87-90 Albert Embankment,
London SE1 7TW
Tel. 020 7339 8500
www.ramblers.org.uk

Yorkshire Dales National Park Authority
Yorebridge, Bainbridge, Leyburn,
N. Yorkshire DL8 3EL
Tel. 01969 652300
Colvend, Hebden Road,
Grassington, Skipton,
N. Yorkshire BD23 5LB
Tel. 01756 751600
www.yorkshiredales.org.uk

National Park Authority visitor centres:
Aysgarth Falls: 01969 662910
Grassington: 01756 751690
Hawes: 01969 666210
Malham: 01729 833200

Reeth: 01748 884059

Pateley Bridge: 01423 711147
Settle: 01729 825192

Yorkshire Tourist Board
Dry Sand Foundry, Foundry
Square, Holbeck, Leeds,
LS11 5WH
Tel. 0844 888 5123
www.yorkshire.com

Local tourist information centres:
Leyburn: 01748 828747

Youth Hostels Association
Trevelyan House,
Dimple Road, Matlock,
Derbyshire
DE4 3YH
Customer Services:
Tel. 01629 592700
www.yha.org.uk

Barney Beck below Surrender Mill

Ordnance Survey maps of the Yorkshire Dales

Explorer maps: OL2 (Yorkshire Dales – Southern &
                         Western areas)
                         OL30 (Yorkshire Dales – Northern &
                         Central areas)

Landrangers: 92 (Barnard Castle)
                         98 (Wensleydale & Upper Wharfedale)
                         99 (Northallerton & Ripon)
                         103 (Blackburn & Burnley)
                         104 (Leeds & Bradford)

Answers to Questions:

Walk 1:   Fossilised shells of creatures that inhabited the warm
               carboniferous seas, under which the stone was formed.
Walk 2:   It was a tether to which bulls were tied for the cruel sport of
               bull baiting.
Walk 3:   Approaching the Lower Falls, slabs in the path tell you that
               – 300 million years ago – in a warm tropical sea – creatures
               lived and died – their bodies forming these rocks.
Walk 4:   It has low walls so as not to impede the panniers carried by
               the pack animals.
Walk 5:   700° centigrade; an information panel in the ruined mill at
               Surrender Bridge describes the process.
Walk 6:   A young cow that has not yet calved.
Walk 7:   It is the grid reference of the village. Check it on the
               Ordnance Survey map.
Walk 8:   Look for a plaque on the northern pillar for the date of its
               construction.
Walk 9:   A pound to hold stray cattle until collected by their owners.
Walk 10:   The dale was once called Yoredale after its river, the Ure,
               but the dale now takes its name from the town of Wensley,
               15 miles downstream.
Walk 11:   Three, one on the bank and two standing in the lake.
Walk 12:   The source of the River Ribble lies in the moors nearby.

Walk 13: Carved on a drinking fountain in the centre of Lofthouse.

Walk 14: The heads of two children, marking the site of the first village school.

Walk 15: They contained heads of water to drive the water mills at Linton.

Walk 16: Take along a pocket field guide to help you identify them.

Walk 17: The chief town of Swaledale, Reeth held a major market, attracting producers and buyers from miles around.

Walk 18: 'Den' is Old English for valley, thus 'the valley of the bucks or deer'.

Walk 19: The building was once a 17th-century inn, and the name poked fun at the elaborate clothing fashions of the day.

Walk 20: It was used by shepherds who gathered to wash their sheep at shearing time.

Hardraw Force

Across the dale to Wether Fell

Crimson Walking Guides

Crimson Short Walks

Pathfinder® Guides

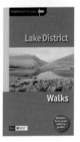

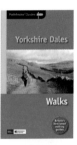

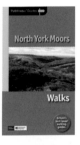

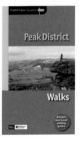

For more information visit www.crimsonpublishing.co.uk
Tel: 020 8334 1600
email: info@crimsonpublishing.co.uk

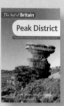